PRINCESS HELENA

PRINCESS HELENA

Queen Victoria's third daughter

John Van der Kiste

A & F

First published by Amazon KDP 2013
Revised and expanded edition published by A & F 2015

A & F Publications
South Brent, Devon, England, UK

Copyright © John Van der Kiste, 2013, 2015

All rights reserved

ISBN-13: 978-1511679206
ISBN-10: 1511679204

Typeset 11pt Roman
Printed by Createspace

Contents

Foreword   3

1. 'Nature certainly divides her gifts strangely' 1846-63   5
2. 'Our good, self-sacrificing Lenchen' 1863-66   17
3. 'Poor dear Lenchen' 1866-77   31
4. 'The want of truthfulness & openness' 1877-90   43
5. 'Violent opinions and very often absurd tirades' 1891-1900   60
6. 'A great comfort to me' 1901-14   77
7. 'My loneliness and desolation' 1914-17   88
8. 'Devoted to humanitarian and to womanly duties' 1917-23   96

Portraits of Princess Helena   102
Illustrations   105
Reference Notes   123
Bibliography   129
Index   135

Foreword

The appellation 'Queen Victoria's forgotten daughter' was originally applied by Gerard Noel in the sub-title of his biography of Princess Alice, later Grand Duchess of Hesse and the Rhine, which was published in 1974. It could equally, if not more so, apply to one of Alice's younger sisters, Princess Helena, sometimes better known by her married name of Princess Christian of Schleswig-Holstein. The latter, like their younger sister Princess Louise, had no legitimate grandchildren and therefore never provided any consorts to European ruling houses. (Unlike her, Louise never had any children either). Moreover, unlike Louise, Marchioness of Lorne and later Duchess of Argyll, her husband never held any posts of major importance at home or abroad.

Uniquely among the Queen's children, she was not initially considered worth an entry in the original 1921-30 supplement to the *Dictionary of National Biography*. It was an omission which I was glad to be asked to make good when it was thoroughly revised and reissued towards the end of the twentieth century as the *Oxford Dictionary of National Biography*. Moreover, while on a visit to Buckingham Palace shortly before I completed the initial draft of this book in 2013, I noticed that the ante-room contained very fine oval portraits by Winterhalter of her four sisters. Helena, it was noticeable, was conspicuous by her absence. A quick look on the Royal Collection website confirmed that there was an equally charming one of Helena in similar format. To have displayed all five might have created some problems of symmetry as regards arrangement on the wall, but even so I was still a little puzzled by the omission.

Helena may have indeed led a comparatively humdrum life, untouched by any major tragedy beyond the untimely loss of two sons, or three, if a stillborn prince is included. Moreover she may not have been a particularly showy personality. One biographer of the family, Nina Epton, wrote that if she had met Queen Victoria's daughters in person and was asked to pass judgement on them, she would probably have found Helena 'dull, but sympathetic in a crisis'.[1]

3

Her importance should certainly not be underestimated. As a tireless worker on behalf of many a charitable cause, she was among the first of many royal princesses who to this day have played an unspectacular and often overlooked but nevertheless invaluable role in the life of the nation, working on behalf of what later royal generations would refer to as 'the firm'.

With the exception of Seweryn Chomet's *Helena: A princess reclaimed* (1998), an interesting and very informative if at times occasionally rather too imaginative study which received a somewhat mixed reception on its appearance, and to an extent the recollections of her younger daughter Princess Marie Louise, *My memories of six reigns* (1956), no publication has yet studied the life of Princess Helena in depth. Her nursing career however has been studied in some depth in Coryne Hall's *Princesses on the wards*. This book, I hope, will go further to shed some light on her life.

My particular thanks go to Sue Woolmans, for the loan of and also direction to much rare and valuable material which I would otherwise have missed; to Ian Shapiro for access to one previously unpublished letter; to Sylvia Hemsil, who proofread the manuscript and made several; valuable suggestions; and to my wife Kim for her invaluable support throughout.

- 1 -

'Nature certainly divides her gifts strangely' 1846-63

'It gives me the greatest pleasure to be able to announce to Your Majesty that yesterday afternoon at 3 o'clock the Queen was safely delivered of a Princess,' Prince Albert wrote to King Frederick William IV of Prussia on 26 May 1846. 'The many proofs of friendship which Your Majesty has given to us assure me that you will receive the news of this gladdening event with your former interest...'[1]

To his brother Ernest, Duke of Saxe-Coburg Gotha, he wrote the same day that 'Heaven gave us a third little daughter. She came into this world rather blue; but she is quite well now. Victoria suffered longer and more than the other times and she will have to remain very quiet to recover from all.'[2]

The Princess was the third daughter and fifth child of Queen Victoria and Prince Albert, who had been married for six years. The Queen had celebrated her twenty-seventh birthday the previous day in some discomfort, and suffered a severe and protracted labour. Also present at the delivery with the proud father were several members of the Privy Council and Ladies of the Bedchamber, with the Queen's mother the Duchess of Kent and others present in the adjoining rooms. Mother and child both made a quick recovery. When this newest arrival was about three weeks old, the Queen noted that she was a 'pretty, fat and most thriving child darker than any of the others and has a great deal of dark brown hair'.[3]

She was christened on 25 July at Buckingham Palace. Two of her sponsors, George, the Hereditary Grand Duke of Mecklenburg-Strelitz, and Augusta, Duchess of Cambridge, were present in person, while the third sponsor, Albert's cousin Hélène d'Orléans, was represented by the infant's grandmother, the Duchess of Kent. Helena Augusta Victoria, the first two names having been chosen after her female sponsors, disgraced herself by crying lustily and sucking her thumb throughout the ceremony. Not long afterwards she made her first appearance in a family portrait. In Franz Xaver Winterhalter's large iconic picture of the Queen, Albert and their elder children, for which sittings began towards the end of 1846, and copies of which now hang at Buckingham Palace and in the dining room at Osborne House, long since familiar through countless reproductions, Helena is clearly visible as the baby who looks out from her cradle at the spectator with questioning eyes.

Her behaviour at the christening would luckily not prove a foretaste of things to come. Princess Helena, or 'Lenchen', short for the German Helenchen, as she was always to be known *en famille*, became a placid, even-tempered child. She had none of the obstinacy or tendency to answer back as was the case with her eldest sister, the precocious, self-willed Victoria, Princess Royal, or the 'cast-down' moodiness of Alice. Despite her easy-going temperament, her two elder brothers, 'Bertie', the Prince of Wales, and 'Affie', Alfred, found out soon enough that she would put up with no nonsense from them, and any attempts at teasing or bullying her would result in a dusty answer. Lady Augusta Bruce, a lady-in-waiting to the Duchess of Kent, was amused to notice that at six years of age the princess 'resented much being called a Baby by her eldest brother and threatened to slap his face if he persisted!'[4]

Only one really serious incident disturbed the peace and calm of Helena's early childhood. A few days before her fourth birthday she, Alice and Alfred were driving down Constitution Hill in a carriage with their mother, when the sound of shots at close range rang out. The culprit was William Hamilton, an unemployed Irishman. His pistol was only charged with powder, and the Queen was shaken but unhurt. 'Man shot, tried to shoot Mama, must be punished,'[5] the shocked little princess murmured afterwards. Hamilton was sentenced to seven years' transportation.

Unambitious and easy-going, Helena had none of her father or her eldest sister's intellectual thirst for knowledge. Yet she was certainly no fool, and did whatever was expected of her at home correctly and neatly if in a rather uninspired way. As a child, everything about her was straightforward and reasonable. With her placid and cheerful manner, her parents and governesses found her much easier to deal with than her more emotional elder sisters and the fourth, Louise, who was almost two years younger than her. With regard to her artistic talent, according to Lady Augusta she could draw at the age of three, but despite this precocious draughtsmanship, her work was generally uneven, and she displayed little feeling for colour.[6] When she was small, embroidery never interested her; it became a family joke that Lenchen was all fingers and thumbs, and that she was the last person they should ever ask to sew on a button. As she began to learn music, she was at first characteristically heavy-handed on the piano, and anybody walking past the music room while she was having her lesson would hear the teacher, Mrs Anderson, repeating patiently, 'Lighter, Princess Helena, lighter.'[7] Although she was a slow developer, she persevered and soon learnt from her mistakes, developing a good ear for and love of music, and becoming a very reasonable pianist and singer. In adult life she would also have a similar passion for needlework.

It was soon evident that Helena never gave up at anything. Her copy-books were always neat and she was quick at arithmetic, and though her essays were inclined to be more plodding than imaginative, she made up for it by the absence of blots and erasures. She knew that Vicky and Alice were more clever than she was, and never felt overshadowed by their superior intelligence as long as nobody was tactless enough to make any comparisons between her and them to her disadvantage. The governesses appreciated that her lack of competitiveness in the schoolroom was a good influence on the others. Never touchy, she was not the kind of girl to set her brothers and sisters against each other, and she could be relied on as a stabilising influence whenever the others quarrelled. What she lacked on the academic and artistic side, she made up for with her love of animals and her practical flair. She could calm a frightened horse much better than the rest of the family; 'unmanageable' horses and ponies bought out a sensitivity and understanding in her that was not always evident in the schoolroom.

When the family went to stay at Balmoral she was in her element. Like her mother she was always impervious to cold and wet weather, and a heavy downpour was no excuse to forego a ride over the hills. Their Scottish Highlands family home was the one where she was always happiest as a child, with Osborne on the Isle of Wight being her second favourite. While her sisters loved cooking in the kitchen and adding new items to the museum in the Swiss Cottage, she preferred to spend her time experimenting with woodwork in the carpentry shop, or joining her brothers in mock battles at their home-made miniature forts.

Of her brothers, only Alfred was naturally mechanically-minded. Being next to each other in age they were close throughout childhood, and Lenchen was almost as good as him when it came to understanding machinery. She enjoyed steering the steam yacht *Fairy* in all weathers, and did so with the calmness of an adult. To her mother's chagrin she was quite uninterested in her appearance, tying her hair back with an old piece of ribbon while she spent hours below deck, getting her hands covered with grease, learning exactly how steam worked. It was her father who championed her against teasing on account of her apparently unladylike, practical ways.

She grew up to be one of the toughest, physically speaking, of the royal sisters. It was hardly surprising that sport appealed to her more than her work in the schoolroom. She was better at swimming than her sisters, and often complained that running races against girls was no fun. When they were at Windsor, she was often to be seen in bitter weather watching the boys at Eton playing football. With her deep voice and long striding gait, and her dislike of trailing around in long skirts, she longed to be an athlete, or at least to lead a more outdoor life. In the dramas and *tableaux vivants* which the children often staged for their parents' amusement, Lenchen generally took the part of a boy. Paintings of the children by Winterhalter usually showed her in Highland dress, with her hair parted at the side like her brothers.

In February 1854, on their parents' fourteenth wedding anniversary, the children performed a *tableau vivant*, representing the four seasons. Princess Alice was Spring, scattering flowers as she delivered a speech from James Thomson's verse drama *The Seasons*. The Princess Royal was Summer, Prince Alfred Autumn, dressed as Bacchus in a leopard skin and crowned with grapes, and the Prince of Wales represented Winter, as an old man warmly dressed up, with icicles hanging from his coat and hat. Princess Louise and Prince Arthur took smaller roles, the latter dressed so scantily that the nurse had to ensure a mildly shocked Queen Victoria that it was all right as he was wearing 'flesh-coloured decencies'. At the closing scene, they gathered in a group with Princess Helena appearing in clouds in a white robe, 'with a long veil hanging on each side down to her feet, and a long cross in her hand'.[8] She then delivered a speech written for the occasion, one assumes by a tutor or governess, in which she proclaimed herself as Christ-loving Helena who had appeared to bless 'this auspicious day and tender their homage to their parents'.

Throughout childhood there are regular glimpses of her in the letters of Lady Augusta Bruce. At the age of six, the Princess was 'so lovely and charming – talks German...making all sorts of neat blunders;'[9] and in Scotland at the age of ten, being helpful and practical. Guests were invited to her grandmother's house at Abergeldie, but she was 'much concerned because the Ladies were not all seated in the drawing room, and offered her services to order chairs to be brought! This Grandmama declined, as with great trouble all those in the house had just been conveyed to the Ballroom!!!'[10] Helena may not have had winning ways, or the gift of her youngest sister Beatrice (the last of the children, born in 1857) for making comic remarks. But as a child she was steady and dependable, and would generally be just as reliable to the end of her days.

When she was eleven, her eldest sister the Princess Royal was married to 'Fritz', Prince Frederick William of Prussia. Helena, like Alice and Louise, took her place as one of the bridesmaids. Now nearing adolescence, her plain looks still did not bother her in the least, even if they were a disappointment to her mother. Soon after her twelfth birthday, the Queen was writing sadly to her eldest sister that 'Lenchen's features are again now so very large and long that it spoils her looks.'[11] That same sister in Berlin was pregnant by this time, and the young future aunt was kept completely in ignorance of the fact by her mother. 'I could not tell such a child as Lenchen about you,' Queen Victoria wrote to Vicky that autumn; 'those things are not proper to be told to children, as it initiates them into things which they ought not to know of, till they are older.'[12]

Only a few days earlier, the Highland ghillie John Brown had almost inadvertently let her into the secret. When she told him that it was Fritz's birthday, he misunderstood her, and according to the Queen he replied, '"Aye! Has she got a girl or a boy?" which startled Lenchen amazingly as she suspects nothing.'[13]

One of the Princess's earliest and most long-lasting friendships she was ever to know during her life was with Emily Maude, daughter of Lieutenant-Colonel George Maude, an equerry to the Queen. The Princess's correspondence with her began in July 1860, when she was fourteen, and continued until within a fortnight of her death some sixty years later. One of the earliest letters was written while the family were in mourning for the Duchess of Kent, who had died of erysipelas at her home at Frogmore on 16 March 1861. The death of her grandmother was 'a very sudden and unexpected blow for us, and we feel it very deeply,' she wrote. 'Mama is I am thankful to say pretty well but she is still very upset and feels the loss terribly; how could we expect it otherwise, the loss of a dear fond parent is a loss which can never be repaired, and day by day Mama feels more the indescribable blank it has made in our family circle.'[14] Helena and the Prince of Wales had been summoned from Frogmore to take a last glance at their grandmother after her death.

If the word of this eldest brother is to be taken at face value, Helena was not yet very mature for her age. The previous year, he had undertaken a tour of Canada and the United States, during which he wrote regularly to Alice. In one of his letters (17 August 1860), he told her what 'a bitter pang' it would be for him to separate from her now that she was engaged to Prince Louis of Hesse, as home would not be the same without her; 'nobody will be able to supply your place, as Lenchen is so much younger and still so childish'.[15] The two siblings obviously still had their differences. Now that Alice was betrothed, they knew it would not be long before she left home.

By this time Helena was aged nearly fifteen, and her childhood was almost over. During the previous year, in January 1860, she had been allowed to attend the state opening of Parliament for the first time. Thirteen months later, she attended the grand dinner at Buckingham Palace which was held to celebrate the twenty-first wedding anniversary of her parents.

Later that year, for the first time, there was talk of a possible suitor for her in the shape of William, Prince of Orange, who had already been considered as a husband for Alice. His rude behaviour on a visit to England, followed shortly afterwards by unfavourable reports about his dissolute character, put paid to any chance of him becoming a son-in-law of Queen Victoria. 'I am vexed to hear people defend that odious Prince of Orange,' the Queen wrote to Vicky, now Crown Princess of Prussia, in Berlin (1 October 1861), 'for they may try to bring him over - and propose him for Lenchen, and whatever other parents may do and think – we never will give one of our girls to a man who has led a life like that young man has done!'[16]

All the same, Helena was at the age when there should be much to look forward to. After the inevitable excitement of being a bridesmaid again, at Alice's wedding, she would be the eldest unmarried daughter at home. Soon after this there would doubtless be a coming-out ball for her, and similar social diversions organised by her parents. Much as Queen Victoria bewailed her lack of beauty, the Prince Consort appreciated that once she 'grew into her looks' she would be handsome if not exactly pretty.

Tragically, an unforeseen blow was about to fall on the family. In the summer and autumn of 1861 Helena accompanied her parents, as well as Alice and Alfred, when they stayed in Ireland for a few days, after which they all went to Balmoral. It was destined to be the last interlude before they returned to Windsor, where the Queen was once again prostrated by grief over the death of her mother, and the Prince Consort, only forty-two years old but prematurely aged by years of overwork, fell ill for what would be the last time. He was already in the grip of raging neuralgia and toothache when he received telegrams in November informing him of the deaths from typhoid of King Pedro V and Prince Ferdinand of

Portugal, two of his beloved Coburg cousins. Helena later told the Archbishop of Canterbury that he felt the King's death so deeply that she never saw him smile again.[17]

After several days during which the Queen alternated between hope and despair, with the doctors reluctant to tell her the very worst, on 14 December the elder children joined her as they gathered round the sickbed at Windsor Castle, Helena sobbing violently behind Alice who sat on the floor at their mother's side supporting her, as the Prince of Wales was standing silently by the sofa. 'Poor Princess Helena could not bear it,' wrote Lady Augusta Bruce. 'The doctors did not like her to be near her father, poor lamb; I did not know what to do with her.'[18]

At ten minutes to eleven, the Prince Consort breathed his last, and the Queen's grief so alarmed the doctors that they feared for her reason. The funeral was held on 23 December, but the Queen had already departed from Windsor with her daughters for Osborne, where they were to spend that joyless first Christmas without the head of the family, so she did not attend. Before they left, she asked each of them to cut off a lock of their hair which was to be placed in the coffin beside the body of their father.[19]

Much of the burden during the ensuing weeks fell on Alice, who took on the task of acting as her comforter and confidante. Helena, suffering further from a bout of neuralgia just after Christmas, unburdened herself to Emily Maude, her 'own precious Emmie' (20 January 1862):

> I think of you daily, oh! When shall I see you again. When shall we have another nice talk together. Oh! all those happy days are over now, and we have only to live on the recollection of them. I am better in health than I was, but I am far from well, sorrow and anxiety do not make one feel well. Oh! Emily if you knew the anguish of my heart. Sometimes, when I think of all I have lost, and that I shall never see in this world again, that dear adored Papa. When I think that all my life will be spent without Papa. But the Almighty in His infinite wisdom has done it all for the best. When I go to bed at night I feel as if my heart would break. One wishes one could sleep all through the day and night.[20]

On 17 April, Helena was confirmed at Osborne. 'Poor dear Lenchen's confirmation; it will be an awful day!'[21] the Queen wrote to the Crown Princess of Prussia. For the elder children, this important rite of passage had been an occasion for celebration, including a table laden with presents, and a large family luncheon afterwards at which she would have been the principal figure. Neither of these privileges was provided for 'poor Lenchen', who wore the simplest of white dresses, and had her catechism in her father's room, still filled with reminders of their loss all around them.

'I got over the solemn day of Thursday quite well, it is impossible for me to describe what I felt, you will know soon,' she wrote to Emily Maude (19 April 1862). 'My fervent prayer is that I may be able to keep the solemn view I have made. It has been one of the most important stages of my life. I am no longer a child, a great responsibility lies on me. May God help me'.[22]

Alice and Louis's wedding was on 1 July 1862, a dismal ceremony held in the dining room at Osborne House. When Alice left England for her new married home at Darmstadt, the main burden now fell upon Helena as the eldest of the daughters left at home. Ironically, it was perhaps her lack of remarkable qualities and sheer commonsense that made her such an able secretary, companion and confidante to her grieving mother.

For a time, nobody dared to be openly cheerful in the Queen's presence, and the slightest sign of merriment would result in a severe scolding. It was bad enough for the children to have lost their father so suddenly, without being expected to demonstrate their misery constantly in order to please their mother. Yet Helena helped to bring a breath of normality into the mourning atmosphere at home. More tactful and less mercurial than Louise, she could get away with much that her younger sister could not. Queen Victoria was quick to appreciate the straightforward qualities of Helena's character. She never bore malice towards her brothers and sisters, and 'never made mischief'. In short, she could always be trusted implicitly by everyone. As the eldest sibling, her diplomatic skills were sometimes required to keep the younger ones in order. The haemophiliac youngest son Leopold, who had just celebrated his ninth birthday, had spent the winter in France on medical advice. When he returned home, he was disappointed to find he was no longer the centre of attention, and he thought that more notice was being taken of twelve-year-old Arthur and five-year-old Beatrice than of him. It took a terse note from Helena to stop him from being unpleasant to their youngest sister. Beatrice, she told him, was 'quite well and so good...she is not a "stupid little thing" as you call her.'[23]

If Helena ever harboured any jealousy of her younger sisters, it would not have been surprising. Louise may have been capricious, but she was extremely pretty and grew up to be the most attractive of the Queen's daughters, in appearance if not in character, while 'Baby' Beatrice's childish sayings captivated the adults. Queen Victoria was frequently making comparisons between the girls; tactless remarks to Vicky on Louise's good looks, and comments such as 'Baby is most amusing and her sayings are charming. Lenchen shall send you an account of them'[24] could not but have inspired envy in the elder sister at home whose 'usefulness' sometimes seemed but scant compensation.

Looking after this demanding and often tactless mother was an exhausting business. 'I hope you forgave me for not having answered you sooner, but I have had to do so much for dear Mama, that it was impossible,' she wrote apologetically to Emily Maude (22 July 1862). 'Do write sometimes if you can, but do not think that I have forgotten you if I do not answer immediately, as I have many new duties to perform since Alice left. I am well, but very tired, and long for rest. These last few weeks, even months I might say, have been so full of bustle, worry, with one thing and another, besides the trial of parting from a Sister, then from a Brother, that I am quite weary.'[25] Although having to support her mother was a burden, she coped with patience and even a sense of humour, guarded though it was. She told Louise how she longed to laugh when the Archbishop of York did homage at a morning council.

Within the family, Helena's greatest friend and help was her eldest sister the Crown Princess of Prussia. Though she lived in Berlin, and had two children of her own to look after, in best 'eldest sister' tradition, she did what she could to act as mother to the rest while Queen Victoria was at her lowest ebb in the first months of widowhood. She took Helena under her wing after their father's death, and invited her to pay frequent visits to Prussia. Full of commonsense, for which some other biographers have failed to give her sufficient credit, Vicky taught her to be more patient with the Queen and her seemingly never-ending grief.

In the autumn of 1862, shortly after Alice's wedding at Osborne House at which Helena and her younger sisters were bridesmaids, Princess Alexandra, the daughter of Prince Christian of Denmark, came to spend a few days with Queen Victoria. Fate had cast her as the future bride of the Prince of Wales, and the Queen was anxious to get to know her well first. Helena was among those who greeted her as she arrived in England, and the two quickly formed a good relationship. '(Alix) and Lenchen adore one another, and seem to suit so well,'[26] the Queen wrote approvingly to Vicky (8 November).

Helena proved useful in helping the artist William Powell Frith the following year when he was commissioned to paint the official group portrait of the Prince and Princess of Wales's wedding which took place in March 1863. Though he was invited to come and portray some of the royalties from life, much of his work had to be done from *cartes-de-visite*, particularly of those who came from European countries and had since returned home. At the age of six, Beatrice was a rather boisterous sitter, until Helena gently recommended to him that he needed to 'overawe' her a little first.

Less easy to overawe was the tiresome four-year-old Prince William of Prussia. 'Mr Fiff, you are a nice man,' the little prince told the artist, 'but your whiskers...' Helena promptly applied a hand gently to her nephew's mouth, whereupon he struggled to remove it and repeated, 'Your whiskers - ' Blushing as she laughed helplessly, she led him to the other end of the room and gave him a gentle lesson in good manners. After that, to try and keep him quiet Frith allotted him a small area of the canvas on which to paint his own picture. All went well until the Prince's nurse noticed with horror that he had been wiping the brushes on his now multicoloured, randomly streaked face. Frith proceeded to grasp his awkward young sitter firmly and administer turpentine to the affected area, until a drop went into his eye and he started screaming violently. 'You nasty Mr Fiff!' be bellowed, giving the artist a hefty kick as he ran to hide under the table.

Frith was particularly taken with Helena and Louise. When the time came for them to sit for the portrait, he thought them charming, and that none of their photographs did them justice. The difficulty he had, he went on, was 'to keep in mind in whose presence you are – they laugh and talk so familiarly, and still sit well.'[27] Helena was equally full of praise for Frith's picture, painted under what were sometimes quite trying circumstances. 'You may say to the public that we are delighted with it,' she told him, 'and beg you never to touch it again; we think it perfect...'[28] The Queen herself was less fulsome, noting in her journal that the likenesses were 'not very good', though a few weeks later she conceded that the painting was 'really a very fine thing.'

One friendship which has given vent to some speculation on the part of previous biographers as to its full extent was that between Helena and Carl Ruland. One of the Prince Consort's German secretaries, appointed to his post in 1859 on the advice of Baron Stockmar, he was a cultured gentleman who also took on the roles of royal librarian and manager of the royal art collection, as well as German tutor to the Prince of Wales and probably the younger children as well. Rumour and fact are difficult to separate, but in modern parlance it appears that Helena may have had something of a teenage crush on this man who was twelve years older than her, and perhaps filled a gap as he seemed like something of a badly-needed father figure after the sudden loss of the Prince Consort. Whether Ruland encouraged and even returned her feelings or not, or whether he was wise enough to treat a temporary infatuation which she would soon grow out of at face value and do nothing, will never be known, but the latter seems more likely. It has been stated that Queen Victoria discovered or was informed that an improper liaison had formed between them, or was about to be, and she angrily dismissed Ruland, sending him back to Germany.[29]

Those who thought they had detected scandal within the walls of Windsor Castle were to be sorely disappointed. In fact he had asked the Queen if he might be relieved of his duties in order to return home to Germany and look after his ailing mother, which he did with her full approval and sympathy in October 1863. He was awarded a pension for his services, while he continued to carry out work in connection with the Prince Consort's collection of works by Raphael, and visited Windsor Castle at least twice on subsequent occasions. All this seems to suggest that it is likely nothing improper ever took place between him and the young princess after all.[30]

Whatever the truth of the matter, tutors and governesses were all too often a potential problem. Earlier that year the Queen had decided to dispense with the services of Madame Hocédé, a French governess. She believed that the woman had been a bad influence on the princesses, and in particular giving Helena and Louise books to read which were not 'suitable'. Louise tried to cover up for her by telling her mother that she had found the books herself, but Mama did not believe her. She awarded the governess a pension and explained to her that as the children were older they did not need three governesses. However, the former employee angered the Queen by telling the children that she had been dismissed.

By now, her help as her mother's constant prop had been acknowledged, albeit tacitly. Writing to Vicky a few days after Beatrice's sixth birthday, the Queen said she was 'the only thing which keeps me alive, for she alone wants me really. She, perhaps as well as poor Lenchen, are the only two who still love me the most of any thing.'[31] When Denmark and Prussia went to war in January 1864 over the disputed ownership of the duchies of Schleswig and Holstein and Vicky sent Fritz's letters from the battlefront to Windsor for Queen Victoria to read, the Queen assured her that only three other adults, and Lenchen, were allowed to see them. The Prince of Wales, whose father-in-law had just ascended the throne of Denmark as King Christian IX and was therefore no champion of Prussia or her interests, was not.

Lenchen was sensible and discreet, but still not perfect. Queen Victoria could not help singing the praises of Louise (23 March 1864), who was 'so graceful and her manners so perfect in society, so quiet and ladylike.' On the other hand, 'poor dear Lenchen, though most useful and active and clever and amiable, does not improve in looks and has great difficulties with her figure and her want of calm, quiet, graceful manners. Nature certainly divides her gifts strangely.'[32] It was left to the Crown Princess, who regularly took on the role of champion of the underdog, to point out tactfully to her mother (26 March) that 'Lenchen cannot help her looks though, poor child, and I think you will see she will grow into them and, though she may never be as pretty as Louise which I do not think she will, still she may be much admired. Grace of manner is also a gift...'[33]

Helena also had another supporter in Prince Alexander of Hesse, whose sons Louis and Henry would in time marry the Queen's granddaughter and daughter respectively. On a visit to England and the royal family around 1864, he wrote to his sister Marie in Russia about his hosts and the children, suggesting that the fourth daughter did not have a monopoly of good looks after all; 'The Princesses Helena and Louise are pretty, especially the former, and look very intelligent.'[34]

Throughout these difficult years, Helena could still count on the close friendship of Lady Augusta Bruce. It came as a considerable surprise to the family when, at the age of forty-one, Lady Augusta announced her engagement to Arthur Stanley, Dean of Westminster. 'May God bless you dearest, and grant you all that happiness which you so richly deserve,' Helena wrote to her (11 November 1863).

> To me you have ever been the best of friends and it is the thought of not so often seeing you that makes me so sad. But this is very selfish in me to say so, but you understand me dearest Augusta. You know how tenderly I love you, how I have always looked up to you for comfort and advice in all my troubles and difficulties. And you always helped me, how am I to thank you for all your kindness and love to me. Pray always remain the same to me, for what should I do without you my ever dear kind friend.[35]

By this time Helena was aged seventeen. Although she was an invaluable assistant to her mother, it was increasingly evident that the matter of her marriage would have to be considered before long.

- 2 -

'Our good, self-sacrificing Lenchen'
1863-66

'A married daughter I MUST have living with me,' Queen Victoria wrote to King Leopold of the Belgians (18 May 1863), in a mood of virtual despair after Alice and Louis had returned to Germany after a visit to Windsor.

> I intend (and she wishes it herself) to look out in a year or two (for till nineteen or twenty I don't intend <u>she</u> should marry) for a young, sensible Prince, for Lenchen to marry, who can during MY <u>lifetime</u> make my house this <u>principal</u> home. Lenchen is so useful, and her whole character so well adapted to live in the house, that (unless Alice lived constantly with me, which she won't) I could not give her up, without <u>sinking</u> under the <u>weight</u> of my desolation.[1]

One year after this letter was written, Helena celebrated her eighteenth birthday. She was as unfailingly 'useful' to her mother as ever. 'Everybody says no Drawing Room without me gave so much satisfaction as the one held by Lenchen,'[2] the Queen wrote to the Crown Princess of Prussia, almost another year later (23 May 1865).

Another valuable role she played was in helping to prepare the first authorised biography of her father. The Queen had asked Lieutenant-General Charles Grey, her private secretary, to compile an account of the life of the Prince Consort from his earliest years to February 1841, their first wedding anniversary. It was initially intended merely for private circulation among the family, but in 1867 a decision was taken to publish *The Early Years of The Prince Consort* for the public, in order to avoid the danger of possible garbled pirate editions. Most of the Prince's letters used in the book were translated by Helena, as Grey noted in his letter to the Queen in March 1866, and reproduced as an introduction, 'with surprising fidelity'.[3]

She was now old enough to begin attending engagements in public. One of the first of these was an appearance at the opening of the Royal Albert Infirmary at Bishop's Waltham, Hampshire, in November 1865, with Louise and Arthur. The old abbey barn was decorated as a concert room, while the ceremony included the unveiling of a statue of the Prince Consort, and readings by the actress Helena Faucit from *The Merchant of Venice*. It was commemorated by a painting by an unknown artist, now in the National Portrait Gallery. Nevertheless she had reached the age when the question of her marriage, albeit under carefully controlled conditions which would preferably not take her as far away from home as her sisters, still had to be considered.

Even before the death of the Prince Consort, it had been hinted that if William, Prince of Orange, could not become betrothed to Alice, then he was prepared to wait for Princess Helena as the next possible bride from Queen Victoria's family. However the Queen was at pains to dismiss any possibility. Two years later the Crown Princess of Prussia, realising from a distance how possessive their mother was becoming of 'poor Lenchen', attempted to make plans for a match between her and 'Abbat', King William of Prussia's nephew, Prince Albrecht. When she was warned that he was planning to come to Britain in order to 'inspect' this possible bride-to-be, the Queen moved rapidly to pour scorn on the suggestion. She may have felt that Vicky wanted to have Lenchen close at hand to act as a kind of assistant, and in any case she had already lost her two eldest daughters to German princes, where they were too far away to act as constant companions and secretaries, and she had no intention of losing her third to the same country. That country would likewise have looked askance on such a scheme. To have two of Queen Victoria's daughters to princes of the royal house of Prussia would have doubtless been unacceptable to the rest of the court at Berlin. The idea that she might be married to Henry of Hesse, brother of Alice's husband Louis, similarly came to nothing. So did the possibility of a match with Duke Elimar of Oldenburg, on whose behalf Queen Augusta of Prussia, the Crown Princess's mother-in-law, made tentative enquiries.

There were also rumours that she was to be engaged to one of the elder sons of King Christian IX of Denmark. Crown Prince Frederick was studying at Oxford and, it was said, had 'conceived an affection' for the sister of his brother-in-law 'which was by no means wholly one-sided'. The Queen commanded General Grey to inform Sir Augustus

Paget, the British Minister in Copenhagen, that he should let it be known 'in a friendly way, but so clearly as to permit of no misunderstanding, that she would never consent to a marriage of any of her daughters with the Crown Prince of Denmark.'[4] The Crown Prince's brother, who had recently become King George of the Hellenes, was also spoken of briefly as a possible bridegroom, though the likelihood of this was likewise never considered seriously. In view of the haste with which the Queen had moved to dispel the notion in 1862 that her second son Alfred should become King of the Hellenes, it was never in the least likely that she would look favourably on the somewhat dubious honour of her daughter becoming Queen Consort.

'Either Lenchen must remain in single blessedness, which would be most unfortunate,' the Queen wrote to King Leopold, 'or we must find someone else.'[5] Princess Helena must be married soon; but it was imperative that she should have a husband who was prepared to make his home in England. He must be sensible, moral, reasonably young, and wealthy enough to support his wife if anything should happen to her mother.

The chance of finding anybody who fitted this description precisely was not surprisingly rather remote. However, at length a candidate who fulfilled some if not all of the criteria was found in the shape of Prince Christian of Schleswig-Holstein-Sonderburg-Augustenburg. He was the younger brother of Frederick, who had proclaimed himself Duke of Schleswig and Holstein on the death of King Frederick VII of Denmark in November 1863 and the accession of Prince Christian as King Christian IX. The latter was only distantly related to his predecessor on the Danish throne, and owed his claim – sanctioned as it was by the London Protocol of 1852 – to the closer relationship of his wife Louise, who had been born a princess of Hesse-Cassel.

The question of the duchies was a complicated one, and the Prime Minister and former Foreign Secretary Lord Palmerston had once said light-heartedly that only three people had ever fully understood it. One was the Prince Consort, now dead, while another was a German professor, who had since gone mad. The third was he himself, and he had forgotten all about it.

Otto von Bismarck, who had been appointed Minister-President of Prussia in September 1862, disputed all the rival claims of all the rival princes. Determined to wrest them from King Christian of Denmark, within a few weeks of the latter's accession in November 1863 he had declared war on behalf of Prussia on their Scandinavian neighbour. Hopelessly outnumbered, the Danes stood no chance against the military might of Prussia and her allies in the German Confederation, and the prize of Prussian victory was to claim the duchies which would henceforth be shared between Prussia and Austria.

Prince Christian was born in January 1831. He would later recall that one of his earliest memories, as a boy of six, was recalling his English nanny entering the nursery in deep mourning, weeping bitterly because she had just heard of the death of her sovereign, King William IV, at Windsor Castle. The tears she shed were not just for the departed sovereign, but also for the young, inexperienced girl of eighteen who was now ascending the British throne. This same girl was now about to become his mother-in-law.

Aged thirty-four, the impoverished Prince Christian was very tall, prematurely balding and with a ponderous manner which made him seem much older than his years. Nonetheless he had a kindly manner, and despite the political differences which made him no admirer of Prussia, he was a close friend of the Crown Prince and Princess, who had openly supported his brother's claim to the duchies. He also had an ardent champion in the shape of King Leopold, who was probably the first person to recommend him to the Queen as a son-in-law.

In April 1865, Queen Victoria asked the Prussian Crown Princess what she thought about Christian, and she replied (18 April):

> You know he is our <u>Hausfreund</u>. He comes and goes when he likes, walks and breakfasts and dines with us, when he is here and we are alone. He is the best creature in the world; not as clever as Fritz [Augustenburg, his brother], but certainly not wanting in any way. He is very amusing when he chooses. We like him very much. He is almost bald;....has a much better figure than his brother, and quite a military <u>tournure</u>.

She added that he was very fond of children and spoke English, and that 'his position here is not an easy or agreeable one.'[6] A less impartial observer might have noted that he 'came and went when he liked' because he had little else to do. By pressing his claim to the hand of her sister, the Crown Princess was well aware that such a marriage would rankle with her eldest brother and do nothing for her own reputation in Prussia. However, where the interests of her mother and sister were at stake, she would not allow herself to be deflected. In her own words she enjoyed 'a pitched battle (when it comes to it) exceedingly'. Her recommendation was good enough for Queen Victoria, and she asked to meet Christian. She too liked him on sight and found him very pleasant to talk to. Admittedly, his love of cigars, estimated at twenty-four a day on average, was a disadvantage.

Moreover there was some truth in the assertion that he did absolutely nothing in his ample leisure time but eat, smoke and shoot birds - but nobody was perfect.

In August several members of the family were present at Coburg, where a statue of the Prince Consort was unveiled amid much ceremony, and Christian was among the guests invited. He was also asked to have lunch with the Queen, and later that week she wrote to King Leopold that she found him 'extremely pleasing, gentlemanlike, quiet, and distinguished. Lenchen (who knows nothing yet) has of her own accord told me how amiable and pleasing and agreeable she thought him.'[7]

In a sense, Christian was already family. He and Helena were third cousins in descent from Frederick Louis, Prince of Wales, the son of George II and father of George III. Moreover, though she might not have welcomed the knowledge, the Princess of Wales was also a third cousin of Christian in descent from Frederick V of Denmark.

On 11 September, the Queen excitedly told her eldest daughter, 'in the very strictest confidence', that there was a genuine prospect of Christian and Helena becoming betrothed. 'You know that Lenchen could not and would not leave me, as in my terrible position I required one of my daughters to be always in England.'[8] Both parties had met in Coburg and had apparently been attracted to each other. While the Queen admitted that the difference in ages – Helena was fifteen years the younger – was a problem, there seemed little doubt that Christian liked her very much, and he had 'entirely accepted' the Queen's conditions.

The Queen also told Queen Augusta of Prussia (17 October 1865) that she had

> the reassuring prospect of having found for our good, self-sacrificing Lenchen a husband who, by virtue of his character, is able to be a support to her, will make her happy, and is prepared to settle in England. This last point has become unavoidably necessary owing to my sad position, if I am to get through my heavy tasks at all. In Prince Christian of Holstein-Augustenburg we believe we have found the right husband. He has made the most favourable impression upon Lenchen, and so has she upon him. Since then he has expressed (though his brother) his lively desire to get to know Lenchen better, in the hope of winning her love, and I have invited him to Osborne for the end of December. Though naturally no engagement has taken place, and cannot take place till they know each other better, yet may I regard the matter as pretty well settled, and that sets my mind at rest. You have known Prince Christian for a long time, so that, as I hear, you have

a good opinion of him. I feel certain that in the circumstances my beloved Albert would approve...⁹

As a young princess from the house of Saxe-Weimar, the future Queen Augusta herself had been more or less forced into a marriage of convenience with the then Prince William of Prussia, a man several years older than she was, with whom she had nothing in common on a personal level. What she thought about the impending marriage, and indeed how she thought about an alliance with a princely house which was at odds with her husband's kingdom, can only be imagined. 'Our good, self-sacrificing Lenchen' was undoubtedly prepared to fall in with the plans being made for her by the elder generation. Never a rebel, she was unlikely to put up any resistance to her Mama's plans. On the contrary, she seemed perfectly content. Never vain, she realised that she was not very pretty, and unlikely to make a particularly dazzling match. Countess Blucher's oft-quoted and somewhat blunt verdict that she was 'wanting in charm'[10] conflicts with the more generous comments made so often about her by the admittedly more partisan Lady Augusta Bruce during her formative years. However, the Countess was a lady-in-waiting of Queen Augusta of Prussia, an ungracious personality at the best of times. Although she had been a friend of Queen Victoria for some time, she was not generally disposed towards most members of the Queen's family, and could thus hardly be regarded as an impartial observer.

As for the Queen's own critical comments about her third daughter, these may have focused on what was thought to be Helena's slightly ungraceful manner and tomboyish characteristics. Even as a young adult she seems to have been the least feminine of the family, still always happiest with the more practical sporting pursuits, mechanical activities or the more 'horsey' side of life – all attributes which were not exactly considered becoming in a Victorian princess. Being obliged to suppress these characteristics and behave as she was expected, it is thought, might have had a somewhat detrimental impact on her character once she was a grown woman.

Being fifteen years older than his intended, Christian may have seemed like something of a father figure. Something of his manner might also perhaps have reminded her of the Prince Consort in some ways. On 1 December he arrived at Windsor, and duly proposed to Helena.

Was it a love match? In the nineteenth century, marriages in the British royal family always had some 'arranged' element. The days of King George III, when he and his courtiers would marry his son off to a totally unsuitable cousin merely so that dynastic duties could be performed, were over. Queen Victoria and the late Prince Albert had not been above applying a little subtle pressure when it seemed that their elder children might have found the right partner for life, but they would never have attempted to coerce them into marrying someone with whom they would clearly be incompatible. It was beyond doubt that the Queen intended to make Helena the wife of a prince who would agree to their making their married home within close distance of her at home in England, and at first glance, the idea that a princess of just twenty years of age could instantly fall in love with someone who was fifteen years her senior might seem a little surprising. Yet they both took to each other well, and it was as close a loving relationship as that of any of her sisters with their husbands. Alice and Louise soon found to their cost that theirs were not exactly suitable as lifelong partners, while Beatrice's own married life would later prove to be sadly short. Only Vicky remained totally and utterly devoted to her husband over thirty years of wedded bliss, a union which was severely tested by the political climate in which they were forced to lead their lives until Fritz's illness and early death.

Once the engagement was made public, the result among Helena's elder brothers and sisters was virtually to create war within the family ranks. Only the Crown Prince and Princess of Prussia, Christian's personal friends, gave the impression of being really pleased at first. Alice objected strongly, on both personal and political grounds; she believed her sister's happiness was being sacrificed to their mother's convenience, and even warned Christian that in marrying her sister he should be careful not 'to be put upon'. Moreover, she knew that the wrath of Berlin would descend on the whole family for so openly championing the brother of the defeated claimant to the duchies. Such a marriage would be regarded by King William and Queen Augusta of Prussia, and the all-powerful Minister-President Otto von Bismarck, as nothing less than a diplomatic insult. That Bismarck had deprived the brothers of their army commissions, property and status would make little difference. While the Crown Princess refused to allow such considerations to make any difference, the more conciliatory, less combative Alice thought otherwise. Misinterpreting her thoughts and opinions, the Queen was furious with her second daughter, remarking that it was 'sheer selfishness to object'.[11]

Prince Alfred and the Queen's cousin George, Duke of Cambridge, both took the side of Alice, although rather less forcefully. The fiercest criticism came from Lady Geraldine Somerset, lady-in-waiting of Augusta, Dowager Duchess of Cambridge, who wrote in withering terms of 'this abominable, disgraceful marriage' with 'a starving German Princeling'.[12] The Prince and Princess of Wales were equally angry, and the Queen had rightly been anxious at the prospect of how they would react. Princes Frederick and Christian had taken the German side during the Prusso-Danish war of 1864 which had culminated in King Christian IX losing so much of his kingdom at a stroke, and the Princess of Wales saw the betrothal as a deliberate insult to her parents and their country. Moreover, she thought it was an indication that Queen Victoria no longer loved or approved of her. 'I cannot say how painful and dreadful it will be to me,' she wrote to Lady Macclesfield, her lady-in-waiting, about 'this charming marriage'.[13]

In addition, unpleasant rumours were circulating around England about Christian. He was said to be a lunatic, he had fifteen illegitimate children, and he was planning to bring one of them with him to live with him and his wife-to-be.

Another odd, if less bad-tempered response, came from John Brown, now the Queen's chief personal Highland servant. He congratulated Helena, adding, 'Only one thing; I hope you'll never forget the good Queen.'[14] Helena could have been forgiven for regarding this remark as little short of impertinent.

The Queen was prepared for opposition among her family and insisted in a letter to King Leopold of the Belgians that she would not allow their attitude to deflect her; after all, she had had to put up with much coldness from Germany when her eldest son and heir's engagement to a Danish princess had been announced. Optimistically, she thought that both of them had taken the news of Helena's impending engagement much better than they could have expected. They 'will of course be much annoyed,' she had already written to Vicky (11 September 1865), 'but that is of no consequence.'[15] Vicky wrote later that month to say how relieved she was to hear that they had taken the announcement well, 'and I hope and trust that in time they will become reconciled to it so that there may be no coldness or discord in the family.'[16]

Despite her elder sister's reaction, Alice remained displeased at the news about her sister's betrothal. She still thought that it had been brought about largely if not solely in order to fit in with their mother's plans rather than the happiness of her sister, and did not hesitate to make her views known. The Queen totally misunderstood her reasoning, reporting bitterly to King Leopold (4 October 1865) how she was grieved 'that Alice cannot conceal her extreme dislike to her sister's settlement in England which is mere jealousy and pains me.'[17]

The Prince and Princess of Wales were even more vehemently opposed for political reasons, and before long the Prince was telling his mother that he felt so strongly about the issue that neither of them could possibly attend the wedding. In addition to the matter of solidarity with his wife and her family, he may have felt jealous that Helena appeared to have their mother's confidence more than he did, and that once Christian was part of the family she would extend this to her son-in-law as well, but not her son and heir. At first he refused to meet Christian, and Helena had to appeal to General Grey to intercede. The Prince of Wales was then persuaded to put personal considerations on one side and gave Christian a none too cordial welcome, but his wife still kept her distance.

This threat of an open rupture to family unity, which had already been strained enough, brought Alice to heel. Though she did not alter her views, she realised that her sister was a more or less willing victim, and looked upon Prince Christian as her last chance of marriage. Having initially been so fiercely opposed, she now changed her mind. Keen to try and restore family unity, she implored the Prince of Wales: 'Don't let you be the one who cannot sacrifice his own feelings for the welfare of Mother and Sister,'[18] particularly as Mama had almost 'broken with' so many of her relations and friends by championing his own marriage. The Crown Princess of Prussia also wrote to her brother to assure him that Helena's marriage was certainly no sign of any change in the Queen's affection for the Princess of Wales; while Alfred wrote soothingly to his brother that

> the engagement has taken place and we must put a good face on it. Of course the relationship is painful to you, but you must try to accept him for what he is worth personally, and don't look at him for what he is worth personally, and don't look at him with a prejudiced eye for he is really a very good fellow though not handsome.[19]

A lack of good looks was not Christian's only problem. Though the Queen was relieved that the rest of her children had come to accept the marriage with good grace, she could not help finding fault with her future son-in-law. On his thirty-fifth birthday, she told the Crown Princess of Prussia (24 January 1866) that 'We think him looking older this time even than last December! And his manners and movements are so old...I think when he has been here sometime he will look fresher and younger.'[20]

A week later, she could report with satisfaction that he was looking younger and better since his arrival, and spending more time in the open air; 'He has plenty of good sense – and will, I am sure, in time take plenty of interest in many things. He and Lenchen seem thoroughly fond of each other, which is a great comfort – much as it tries me to feel my own child's affections are now entirely divided.'[21]

The Queen resolved to take this next son-in-law firmly in hand. After their first meeting, she said that she would do something about his cough and teeth,[22] was determined that he should spend plenty of time outside 'not coddling himself', take English lessons, and learn how to make a speech in public. She was reassured by the loyal verdict of General Grey, who considered that he could not praise Christian too highly: 'His tact and good feeling about everything, and above all his good sense and sound judgement cannot be compared.'[23] Christian was doubtless wise enough to appreciate that tact would be a necessity in marrying into a family which had been so divided about acquiring him as a member.

The Queen had been avoiding public appearances since the death of the Prince Consort. Nevertheless some tasks had to be done, and on 6 February 1866 she came before Parliament, somewhat nervously, to announce officially her consent to the marriage of her third daughter. The union, she said, would she hoped be 'prosperous and happy'[24] and she requested an annuity and dower for the bride. By an Act of Parliament dated 23 March, an annuity of £6,000 and a dower of £30,000 were granted. In addition the Queen provided a capital investment of £100,000, yielding an income of £4,000 per annum.[25]

Helena was very contented, and looking forward to some sense of freedom. As the Queen had rightly foreseen, though the young couple would be living close to her, at least her daughter would no longer be completely at her beck and call. 'These last six months have brought me such real happiness that I do indeed look forward to a very bright happy future with my Christian,'[26] she wrote to Emily Maude (26 May 1866).

Some thought that there would not be a bright happy future after all. In May, the London correspondent of the Dublin newspaper *Saunders' Newsletter* reported that 'a strange rumour has gradually obtained considerable currency in society here' to the effect that the wedding would not take place.

> By some it is asserted that increased intimacy has developed an incompatibility of disposition between the affianced couple, and that it is from the doubt as to her future happiness that this startling resolution has emanated. Others, however, declare that certain incidents in the previous life of the illustrious bridegroom – though casting no stain upon his honour – are such as, in the eyes of an august personage, render it inadvisable that the contemplated union should be accomplished. I have very carefully endeavoured to ascertain the truth or fallacy of this rumour, but I have succeeded

only in discovering that it at least certainly exists on a far more extended scale than I had any idea of.[27]

The 'august personage' was presumably Queen Victoria, but 'strange rumour' the story remained, and no more.

On the whole, for the family, it would not prove to be a good summer. In June Prussia declared war on Austria and her allies in the German Confederation, including Hesse, in order to settle the question of the administration of Schleswig and Holstein for once and all. The Crown Princess's unhappiness that war could not be averted turned to grief when the doctors left for the battlefront with the Crown Prince, and there were none left at home when her twenty-one months-old son Sigismund fell ill with meningitis and died in agony. On 3 July the Prussian army won an overwhelming victory on the battlefield of Sadowa (Königgrätz). As a result of the peace terms which followed, the Grand Duke of Hesse and his family, including Alice, were left close to bankruptcy.

Added to such unhappiness was a bone of contention. Who was going to give the bride away at the wedding? As far as the Queen was concerned, as mother and sovereign, she intended to break with tradition and do so herself. When some members of the family, notably Crown Prince Frederick William, expressed surprise at her doing so and thought one of the bride's elder brothers should be performing this role, she explained firmly that she was the only one who could. Ernest, Duke of Saxe-Coburg, was in effect the male head of the family, and if he had been attending, he would have been an obvious choice.

Nevertheless she was still determined to give her daughter away; 'I never would let one of my sons take their father's place while I live.' The rumours in Germany that neither the Prince of Wales nor the Duke of Edinburgh were doing so indicated their disapproval of the marriage were 'a monstrous invention – like everything else printed at that time.'[28] The bride and her mother had agonised over the decision to do so, and in February Helena had written to Lady Augusta Stanley, saying how anxious Mama had been at the possibility that there might have been an *actual* bar against it', but 'she says as she is the Sovereign and does the work of man and is in a peculiar position now, that she does not see why she cd. not do it as well as she sits on a throne and does so many things wh. a man does'.[29]

Helena's twentieth birthday, and her last before her wedding, was celebrated in the Orangery at Windsor. It was a tea dance for the children of the servants, and continued until about 7.40 p.m. After that the royal children joined the Queen for dinner, which finished with a toast to

Helena proposed by nine-year-old Beatrice. A little later Helena and her friend Louisa Bowater, daughter of a late groom-in-waiting to the Queen, went for a drive together around Virginia Water. Her forthcoming marriage was naturally the main subject of conversation, and Louisa was probably one of the few close companions to whom Helena felt she could speak candidly. In her diary afterwards, she observed that the princess spoke to her 'in simplest and most natural way of her affection for Prince Christian'.[30] It was perhaps significant that the word affection, but not love, should have been mentioned.

On 30 June it was announced in the *Gazette* that Prince Christian, who had hitherto been merely a Serene Highness and an officer in the Prussian army, had been 'declared and ordained' by Her Majesty with the style His Royal Highness, and had been appointed a Major-General in the Army, an appointment which, like the marriage itself, was not without controversy. He arrived at Dover on 2 July, spent the night at Buckingham Palace, and accompanied by the Duke of Edinburgh travelled to Windsor next day as a guest of the Queen, to be received by Her Majesty and her daughters at the principal entrance to the castle.

Much to her regret, the Crown Princess was unable to come to England and attend her sister's wedding which was taking place at such an inopportune time. When she had asked what Lenchen would like for a wedding present, eighteen-year-old Louise, who was already developing an acid wit, suggested that their sister 'like Herodias should ask for B[ismarck]'s head!'[31]

The wedding took place on 5 July, in the private chapel at Windsor, with the initial procession entering to the strains of Beethoven's *Triumphal March*. Once all the guests had arrived and were making their way to their seats, the Duke of Cambridge was stricken with an attack of gout that caused a short amount of disturbance. Attired in the uniform of a Major-General of the British Army, Christian entered the chapel with his brother Frederick and Prince Edward of Saxe-Weimar. According to *The Times* correspondent, the bridegroom was 'a tall, military-looking man...with a good forehead, but the lower part of his face covered by a beard – such portions of the features are visible wearing a calm, determined expression that never forsakes them, but appears to enter into and influence all his actions'.[32]

To the sound of Mendelssohn's march from *Athalie*, they reached the altar, attended by the Chamberlain and Vice-Chamberlain, Lord Sydney and Lord Castlerosse. Next, as Handel's *Scipione* was played, the bride appeared in white satin decorated with Honiton lace, her dress and train trimmed with knots of orange blossom, myrtle and ivy, with a Honiton lace veil worked in a pattern of myrtle, ivy and rose. She was escorted down the aisle by Queen Victoria, in black moiré embroidered with silver. They were followed by the Prince of Wales in the scarlet uniform of the 10th Hussars, the Duke of Edinburgh in naval uniform, Princes Arthur and Leopold in Highland dress, then Louise and Beatrice. Next came the bridesmaids and train bearers, all unmarried daughters of dukes, marquises and earls, namely Lady Margaret Scott, Lady Laura Phipps, Lady Mary Fitzwilliam, Lady Muriel Campbell, Lady Caroline Gordon Lennox, Lady Albertha Hamilton, Lady Alexandrina Murray, and Lady Ernestine Edgcumbe. On entering the chapel the bride, it was noticed, 'was visibly agitated, but regained composure upon reaching her place at the left side of the altar.'[33] Louisa Bowater noted critically that the Queen looked 'plain and not graceful', but the bridegroom was 'pre-eminently sensible – they very thing for [Helena's] generous, impetuous nature, - and he is extremely kind-hearted, and most universally liked.'[34]

After the ceremony the procession left to Spohr's *March* from *The fall of Babylon*. A private luncheon for the royal family was held in the Oak Room at Windsor, and shortly after four o'clock the bride and groom left by special train for Southampton en route to Osborne where they would spend the first week of their honeymoon.

Several additional honours were bestowed on Christian on their wedding day. The Queen conferred on him the Order of the Garter, and appointed him Ranger of Windsor Great Park, a post that had been established in 1601 to oversee the protection and maintenance of the park, which had been vacant since the death of the Prince Consort.

Family hostilities over the match had evidently not ceased altogether. The Queen reported to the Crown Princess two days after the ceremony that 'certain relations (an old Aunt especially) made one uncomfortable.' The 'old Aunt' was Augusta, the widowed Duchess of Cambridge, with whom the Queen had never been on the best of terms. However she was pleased and relieved that 'Bertie was very amiable and kind', and that 'There were great crowds and great enthusiasm.'[35]

On the afternoon of 13 July, eight days after the wedding, the newly married couple embarked on the royal yacht *Victoria and Albert* to sail for France, and arrived at Cherbourg that evening en route for Paris, Genoa and Interlaken. The Queen had 'excellent accounts ...all but the heat which is such as to almost prevent them going about.' As she observed, 'good Lenchen' had been more fortunate than her two eldest sisters in being 'able to live in this blessed and peaceful land, safe from all wars and troubles.'[36]

She had sorely missed her daughter, who had been so invaluable during a recent ministerial crisis, when she had acted as an intermediary between the Queen, General Grey and the politicians. This was at the same time as she was arranging things for her wedding; 'she really was admirable in her entire unselfishness and anxiety for me – forgetting herself.' Helena was indeed proving a treasure, and the Queen knew that once she and Christian were back from their honeymoon, she would surely never be deprived of help from this most unselfish of daughters again.

- 3 -

'Poor dear Lenchen'
1866-77

When the newly-married Helena and Christian left Switzerland they returned to France, and they spent the next few days of their honeymoon staying at the British Embassy in Paris. Sailing from Boulogne early on 27 August, they arrived at Folkestone later that day on board the *Vivid*. By the evening they were at Windsor Castle, where a suite of rooms had been fitted up in York Tower for their reception. Three days later they left the castle to travel northwards and join the Queen at Balmoral.

Half a century of unstinting support as husband and wife to the royal family lay ahead of them. Where the dutiful daughter of a demanding matriarch was concerned, it would not always be the easiest of burdens to bear.

The first married home of the Christians, as they would always be referred to in the family, was Frogmore House, Home Park, Windsor. Built in the late seventeenth century, it was later acquired by Queen Charlotte, the consort of King George III, as a retreat for herself and her unmarried daughters. On her death in 1818 it passed to her eldest spinster daughter, Augusta, and when the latter died in 1840 Queen Victoria gave it to the Duchess of Kent, who lived there until her death in 1861. They were granted a parliamentary annuity of £6,000 per annum, in addition to a dowry or gift of £30,000, plus £100,000 from Queen Victoria. The sovereign intended to make sure that Helena remained as 'useful' as ever, and did not live too far away.

Much as Helena and Christian had enjoyed their travels abroad, she was particularly glad to be back in England, and especially pleased that unlike her elder sisters they would both be making their home in the land of her birth. 'There is such a feeling of happiness after a long journey of returning to one's house,' she wrote to Emily Maude, 'and I feel deeply the blessing of not having to exchange my own old house for one in a foreign land.'[1]

In the immediate aftermath of the Prince Consort's death, the Queen and some members of the royal household had considered her unreliable because of a tendency to burst into emotional tears. It was hardly an uncommon characteristic of her children, and, in time, her grandchildren as well. (If Helena proved more susceptible to this than other members of the family, it might have been a symptom of the depression that plagued her throughout much of her life, something which was almost certainly not recognised properly by others at the time). They planned to select the younger but more resilient, self-contained Louise for the role instead. However, before long Louise would prove a rather headstrong, Bohemian soul, less easily intimidated and not quite so imbued with the same sense of duty. Mama then concluded that Helena, an 'Angel in the House',[2] was the more obedient, steady one, inclined to be frightened of her mother and put her first, thus better suited to be her assistant with minor secretarial tasks such as writing letters and helping with political correspondence.

Naturally, she soon had her own family to look after. She and Christian became parents for the first time on 14 April 1867, ten months after the wedding, with the birth at Windsor of a son whom they named Christian Victor. He was followed by Albert on 26 February 1869. Next came two princesses, Helena Victoria, generally known within the family as 'Thora', born on 3 May 1870, then Marie Louise on 12 August 1872. All four children were healthy, in particular Marie Louise, whom the proud mother reported to Emily Maude, was at four weeks old 'a great big fat Child and a great love.'[3] Her husband had been mildly disappointed that the new child was another daughter, as her brother Leopold wrote to Louise (22 August 1872); 'Christian regretted that it wasn't a boy, what an old fool!'[4] When Marie Louise was christened in the Royal Chapel, all of the Park employees were invited to attend.

Now that Helena and Christian had four children, Frogmore was too small for them. Moreover, the doctors thought that it was too low-lying, and the poor state of the drains was not considered conducive to good health. It was decided to move them into Cumberland Lodge, which had just been largely rebuilt after being severely damaged in a fire in November 1869. A seventeenth-century former hunting lodge nearby, it was the traditional residence of the Ranger of Windsor Great Park and his family, and the family moved there in July 1872. After paying them a visit with Alice and Beatrice at the end of the following year, Queen Victoria recorded in her journal that Lenchen and Christian had received them, 'and took us over their rooms below and upstairs, which are beautifully arranged with their things from Frogmore, as well as new ones they have got. They really are splendidly lodged.'[5] A little less than a year later Sir Francis Seymour, a groom-in-waiting, noted in a letter to his wife that the house was charming, 'everything quite new (at the Queen's expense) and in very good taste.'[6]

As Ranger of Windsor Park, Christian's duties were hardly onerous. He did however succeed in putting down a plague of frogs one summer at, ironically, Frogmore, on the advice of naturalist Frank Buckland, who suggested that he should obtain more ducks to eat them. He was also given the largely honorary position of High Steward of Windsor, merely requiring attendance at meetings from time to time. To these he generally sent his apologies, or merely absented himself, preferring to go hunting, shooting, alternately feeding his pigeons or playing with his dogs. When one of them ran off, or became ill and a vet had to be called, he was always particularly anxious. Sometimes, particularly in later life, it was said that his animals seemed more important to him than his family.

Living the quiet retiring life of an English country gentleman, or at any rate English by adoption, suited him well. It was said that he was rarely happier than when trudging through coverts, gun on shoulder, in the countryside around Windsor and Osborne, or riding straight to hounds. The walls of Cumberland Lodge were hung with family portraits and pictures of horses and other animals, including several by George Stubbs, as well as hunting trophies and antlers of stags which he had brought down. Most of the furniture was mahogany, with comfortable chairs and embroidered cushions, well-packed bookshelves, curios, knick-knacks, and flowers arranged everywhere. A magazine article on the home life of the 'Christians' observed that marriage had made him 'curiously English' in disposition, tastes, habits and appearance, that he led 'a placid, pleasant life, always gracefully ceding the first place to his amiable and clever wife,' and that as a self-effacing individual, he 'avoided the minor worries which so frequently accompany a career of which a desire for personal aggrandizement is the dominant motive'.[7]

Even so, some people might have been forgiven for thinking that he led too easy a life, perhaps even a dull one. The ever-busy, not to say controlling, Queen Victoria was known to vent her impatience on him. One morning when he was a guest at Osborne she looked out of the window, noticed that he seemed to be pottering about aimlessly in the garden, and sent a message that he ought to occupy himself with something, or else ride somewhere. She might have observed that the latter was a more likely option, as he had little else to do. Sir Henry

Ponsonby, her private secretary, thought that she was 'terribly bored' with Christian, and could not understand why her daughter liked him. 'Besides, he is bald and fat and it's nonsense their being so affectionate with each other.'[8]

There may have been an element of jealousy involved. Christian's life of leisure and ample time to indulge his sporting interests could have been an unintentional reminder to his mother-in-law that the Prince Consort's lifespan had been sharply reduced by overwork and subsequent ill-health. A peaceful if arguably tedious existence with few, if any, really onerous or stressful duties was evidently the way to a long and healthy life, and that Christian had barely a day's illness until the last few years leading up to his death at the age of eighty-six is significant. With the exception of Queen Alexandra, none of the other children-in-law of Queen Victoria would ever live to the age of seventy.

Helena and Christian brought their children up very simply. From an early age they dressed themselves and had to tidy their own rooms. Their playmates were children of the household and of workers on the estate. Christian was a kind and caring father, who enjoyed the company of the youngsters. He loved poetry, knew the whole of Thomas Gray's 'Elegy in a Country Churchyard' by heart, and inspired the children with his enjoyment of literature, as well as telling them stories and teaching them reading and German. Every evening he invited them downstairs to library, where they would sit with him, one on each knee and one on each arm of the chair. He would set them small simple homework tasks and give them weekly examinations on what they had or should have just learned. For the children's tutor they appointed the poet F.W. Bourdillon, who was soon struck by the boys' intelligence and the general mutual affection between the family.

While Queen Victoria and her children had a duty to appear impartial, it was inevitable that some should show a degree of political bias. The Queen's two eldest daughters were generally liberal in their sympathies, and like the Prince of Wales they had a considerable respect for W.E. Gladstone, four times Prime Minister, which their mother never had. Helena's politics inclined towards Conservatism, with a capital and a small C, and she was very much a partisan of Benjamin Disraeli, who became Prime Minister for the first time in February 1868. Lady Augusta Stanley spent some time at Osborne that spring, when she reported that the Princess was 'quite mad about politics – <u>for</u> Dizzy and against Gladstone'.[9] It was by no means a momentary dislike. Some sixteen years later, when the latter's government was sending forces to Egypt and the Sudan, she wrote to Sir Theodore Martin, the official biographer of the Prince Consort, that her 'own fury with Mr Gladstone & Co. knows no bounds.'[10]

During the months that followed the wedding, Queen Victoria was still irritated by the behaviour of one of her daughters. By January 1867 she was ready to forgive Alice for her ill-judged comments prior to the marriage but, as she wrote to the Crown Princess of Prussia, 'she injured herself by the way in which she spoke to many people about Lenchen and her remaining in England – and made great mischief with Louise, and both her brothers.' She had compounded these sins by originally recommending Christian as 'so amiable' as well as being a suitable husband for Helena, then soon after that 'abusing' him, speaking unkindly of Helena and writing bitterly to her. Alice, she concluded, was 'irritable and sharp', not strong, and probably suffering from post-natal depression after 'those large children so quick one another', a process which she had evidently found very trying.[11] When Alice came to stay at Windsor in June 1868 the Queen was pleased and relieved to find that old wounds seemed to have healed, and that everything was 'most comfortable between her and Lenchen.'[12]

It was inevitable that sooner or later such a critical mother as Queen Victoria would not be long in finding fault with her third daughter. After the birth of her second son Albert in 1869, the Queen thought that she had aged badly, with her 'nerves' in a poor state for an unusually long time. Within a couple of years after that, her constant ailments were giving cause for irritation if not concern, with 'cold upon cold, and unbecoming stoutness', something which one feels the increasingly plump Queen was hardly qualified to criticise. Christian, she added, pampered her 'and does not understand in the least how to manage her.'[13] One year later came the unflattering maternal remark that on her twenty-sixth birthday, Helena 'looks much older'.[14] Another reason for the Queen's criticism, of Helena and Louise, was that in her view they were too active and went to bed too late. 'You younger sisters are always moving and sightseeing,' she wrote to Louise (26 January 1872); 'and I think that this is why you are so far less strong than the elder ones, who besides have always kept such early hours.'[15] She had evidently forgotten that as a young woman she too had once had an unquenchable appetite for late nights, until it was sharply curbed after marriage by her easily fatigued husband.

Nevertheless the Queen still found Helena 'useful', and she must have been grateful that Mama was still relying to some extent on her sister Louise as a regular assistant. In the summer of 1870 Louise was betrothed to John Douglas Campbell, Lord Lorne. At one time it had appeared that she was about to become the wife of a Prussian prince, but such an arrangement would not have been popular in the country, and Louise was far too strong-willed to marry into the Hohenzollerns. Having seen the fate of their eldest sister Vicky, she would never have contemplated such an arrangement.

Helena urged Louise not to make any hasty decisions, and advised her to get to know all the eligible suitors first. At the same time she advised the Queen that Louise was indispensable, as Beatrice, aged thirteen at the time, was too young to take her place as an assistant. To some it may have seemed like selfishness on her part, but with a husband and family to look after she wanted her own life, without being at the constant beck and call of a mother who was undeniably very generous when it came to financial provision but ever demanding, and she must have been grateful that there were younger sisters there to ease the everlasting burden.

That same time, during the Franco-Prussian war, the royal family were once again divided. The government remained firmly impartial. In public the Queen supported this, but privately she championed the German cause, albeit with some misgivings. Helena and Christian were wholeheartedly pro-German, and Christian desperately wanted to enlist in the German army so that he could go and fight 'as a good German'. Queen Victoria sympathised with his view, but as Britain was officially neutral and as he was her son-in-law, she explained to the Crown Princess, 'it was thought better he should not, as it might lead to difficulties and complications.'[16] The Prince of Wales was passionately pro-French, a stance which created some temporary problems with his eldest sisters.

The war gave Helena an excellent opportunity to serve her country in a different capacity. As England herself was not at war at the time, it would have been considered inappropriate for her to take up active nursing. Instead, she was glad to be able to put her organisational skills to good use. A few days after the outbreak of hostilities, Colonel Robert Lloyd-Lindsay, later Baron Wantage, published a letter in *The Times*, calling for a National Society for Aid to the Sick and Wounded in War to be established in Britain, following the example of other European countries. To this end a committee of twenty-two members was founded under the chairmanship of the Colonel, with Queen Victoria as Patron and the Prince of Wales as President. Greatly moved by the loss of life and suffering, Helena became Chairman of the Ladies' Committee, which also included her sister Louise, and her second cousin Mary Adelaide, Duchess of Teck.

The Committee appealed for and received donations of money and gifts. Among the items they requested were smelling salts, concentrated meat essence, and iron bedsteads. The Duchess of Sutherland gave a large quantity of linen, Queen Victoria some flannel bandages and pillowcases, and Helena's sister Louise some clothing. Large sums of money were also sent in, and by September 1870 the committee had collected almost £200,000. A decision was made to give £20,000 each to France and Prussia towards the nursing of their sick and wounded. In appreciation of her efforts, Helena was awarded the Bronze Cross of the French Red Cross Society. Determined to learn more, she went on to attend the ladies' classes of the St John Ambulance Association in Windsor, and received a framed certificate for proficiency.

Neither Helena nor Christian would be noted for their good looks as adults, and the same had to be said of at least one of their children. At four months of age little Marie Louise was 'strong, healthy and good-humoured' as well as sitting up like a much older child, but 'is excessively plain and quite unlike the others.'[17] Less than a year later, in October 1873, the Queen was complaining that Helena was becoming touchy and easily offended, partly owing to her health 'and partly from Christian's inordinate spoiling and the absence of all actual troubles and duties', which made it very difficult to live with her. 'She won't either do anything to get better and says she don't care if she is ill or well!! – which is a great mistake.'[18]

In common with many people of the age, Queen Victoria showed a noticeable lack of understanding of her third daughter. In her impatience she thought Helena was a persistent hypochondriac who was being encouraged to exaggerate her ailments by a doting, over-sympathetic husband. Some of her problems, from early in her married life, were certainly physical. Only four years after her wedding, she was becoming a martyr to rheumatism and pain in her joints, and one year later 'congestion in her lungs' was reported.

Less understood were her psychosomatic afflictions. The bereaved Queen was all too often impatient of other people's 'low moods', even when her own closest relations were the sufferers. Unless Helena was really exaggerating her ill-health, Christian was arguably doing no more than carrying out his wedding vows as a fully supportive husband.

Helena, it was thought, being generally of a placid disposition, was inclined to accept her mother's regime in being reluctant to let her daughters run their own lives rather more stoically than her brothers and sisters. Maybe she was better than them at disguising her true feelings than they were, for the sake of peace. Nevertheless, repressing herself in this way was probably one of the reasons for her persistent ill-health, as noted in the diaries of Emily Loch,[19] who was appointed her lady-in-waiting in 1882. Over the years, she seems to have given in to her feelings of being 'overdone', 'very tired', 'voiceless' or merely 'suffering' too much for her disapproving mother's liking. At such times she would retire to bed early, or else stay in bed until noon, but within twenty-four hours later she would be perfectly all right again.

The precise nature of her problems has never been explained, but it is thought to have been a result of physical and psychological problems, sometimes exacerbated by so-called cures.[20] However her mother seems to have cast a long shadow over her life, until the last few weeks when she was too elderly and infirm to strike terror into the heart of her daughter. Even into middle age, Helena did not dare spend a night in Buckingham Palace without having asked the Queen's permission, as to do so would inevitably lead to a right royal rebuke. Moreover, Helena never ceased to be particularly hurt when she heard some of the Queen's unkind and tactless remarks about her, and it was thought that this was one of her reasons for going abroad regularly, as such comments rarely if ever crossed the North Sea to disturb her equanimity when she was in continental Europe.

Poor Marie Louise, who would grow up to be one of the least good-looking members of British royalty, was never to be noted for her good looks. When she was two years old, Helena was advised by the physicians to take 'a change of air' and spend part of the winter in France. Christian accompanied her, and the children were left to stay with their grandmother at Osborne. To reassure them that all was well she sent them a telegram, 'Children very well, but poor little Louise very ugly.'[21] When she was old enough to be told about it, the princess was justifiably put out by such tactlessness, thinking that it was hardly right for the French postal authorities to be informed that the Queen of England had an ugly granddaughter.

This harsh judgment was very much at odds with the words of Benjamin Disraeli, who was admittedly renowned for his flattery. He used to be a regular guest at Cumberland Lodge, and in 1876 he had written to his companions Lady Chesterfield and Lady Bradford that he 'never saw children better brought up; they are engaging - & they are pretty; I dislike ugly children.'[22] Unlike his sovereign, he clearly did not find Marie Louise or her sister unattractive. Sadly, though, they were terrified by him when they were first brought down to meet him. Reminiscing years later, Marie Louise was not sure whether it was the curl on his forehead, or his trying to take them on his knee that put them off him the most. But they shrieked with rage at the sight of him, were promptly sent out of the room and upstairs and in disgrace, where they were given a good scolding.[23]

The Prime Minister was not always enthusiastic about his visits to the house. After spending the particularly cold Easter of 1876 there, and finding the food particularly tough, he left a day earlier than planned. He did however acknowledge that his hosts had been 'kind and good'. He was also a great admirer of Christian who, he said, 'combined tact with a deep, slow-moving mind,' was 'both sensible and good-natured,' and 'a shrewd, sagacious man'.[24] Other people found Christian dull and his interests very limited. They may not have made due allowance for the fact that he was always self-conscious about his strong German accent and his imperfect grasp of the English language.

For much of the time, Helena and Christian lived a relatively peaceful and contented life. Having become particularly fond of music, it was no surprise that the singers such as Jenny Lind, 'the Swedish nightingale', and Clara Butt were among her personal friends. Jenny Lind sometimes sang to the children, although they doubtless did not appreciate that she was one of the major names in her field. One day she came up to youngsters' schoolroom, saying she would like to sing to 'the dear children', which she did. They listened attentively, but after she had finished, little Marie Louise went up to her and asked, 'Dear Madame Goldschmidt, must you always make such a noise when you sing?' The unappreciated performer magnanimously kissed her as she murmured, 'Sweet child'.[25]

Jenny Lind was the wife of Otto Goldschmidt, who founded the Bach Choir in 1875. Made up of amateurs, the choir practised nearly every week at the South Kensington Museum. Helena, who had been a founder member, sang regularly with them and was involved in their management. They had several friends in Windsor who also belonged and would travel to and from London together by train for rehearsals. This helped to lead to her involvement in various charity concerts in and near the capital. For several years on Boxing Day, she played the piano at benefit performances held at Hackney Wick.

In 1876 Helena and Christian broke with royal tradition by sending their sons to a local school, the first royal children to do so. They went initially as day boys and then as boarders, their parents insisting that they should not receive any special treatment. In 1881 Christian Victor went to Wellington College, and in 1884 his brother Albert became a pupil at Charterhouse.

Christian Victor was a quiet, unassuming young man. According to those who knew him well, it often seemed as if he was rather uncomfortable with his status as a prince. From boyhood he shared a love of music with his mother. When he went on to join the army he compiled a collection of music for the band, and asked his mother to look out for new scores to broaden their repertoire. They also shared a concern for the welfare of soldiers' families, and she adopted many of his suggestions and ideas in her work for the Soldiers' and Sailors' Help Society, of which she was President.

Helena's interests in schools went further than merely ensuring that her children received a good education. In 1868 she became a patron of the Adult Orphan Institution, in 1874 President of the Ladies' Committee, and President of the organisation in 1879. Established in 1820 for the orphaned daughters of members of the forces and the clergy, the first royal patron was Princess Augusta, daughter of King George III and Queen Charlotte. When she assumed the post of President, the name was changed to the Princess Helena College for Young Ladies. At the time it was located at St Andrew's Place, Regent Park, moved to Eaton Rise, Ealing in 1882, and some years after her death to Preston, near Hitchin, Hertfordshire.

Helena was pleased to continue the royal tradition and follow in the footsteps of her great-aunt, but she was to prove herself no mere rubber-stamp figurehead. She took an intense businesslike interest in the institution, especially redecoration and provision of suitable furniture and equipment, and she always expected agendas and minutes of meetings to be available for consultation. Her royal status ensured that there would always be authority behind any requests for what needed to be done. During her period of office, she presided over seventy meetings of the school's council, and contemporaries said that she effectively functioned 'as her own Chairman of the Governing Council and Committee, and in some ways also as her own, long-range, Headmistress-Bursar, with a Lady Superintendent on the spot, as her Right-Hand Woman'. Her role in helping with funding campaigns, her approach to school management, and her support of a gradual liberalisation of the school regime were all appreciated by those who worked with and under her.

In later years, one of 'her girls' thought that she was 'a dowdy, dumpy old lady – like an imitation of Queen Victoria'.[26] Women, it is said, often become increasingly like their mothers with age, and Helena was unsurprisingly no exception. She was also very like her mother in having a no-nonsense approach to seeing that things were done.

Helena's first four children were all strong enough and survived to adulthood. Sadly this was not the case with the two youngest. Harald was born on 12 May 1876 'after a severe time', but never throve. Dr Fairbank wrote to the Queen, 'saying how much poor Lenchen had suffered & that the child had been nearly lost.' Two days later she and Beatrice visited the parents at Cumberland Lodge, 'to see the Baby, such a splendid child, & then to dear Lenchen, whom I never saw looking better, or more cheerful.' For a few days the baby appeared to be holding his own, but he then suddenly lost his fight for life.

Queen Victoria was on her way to Balmoral on the morning of 20 May when she was handed two telegrams. One, from the doctor, reported that the child had been improving 'but then most violent convulsions came on, from which the poor dear little Baby never rallied, & died quietly at 7.25.' The other, from Christian, read, 'Our darling little boy was taken from us this morning. Lenchen bears up pretty well.' The Queen, 'dreadfully grieved & upset', was 'so distressed about my now poor darling Child, fearing it might do her harm, though I hope not. All in 2 days, this joy & happiness turned to such bitter grief!....Could think of nothing else but this sad event & kept constantly seeing the sweet little Infant before me, which I then thought was recovering! May God support my poor dear Child.'[27]

Although the Princess of Wales had not always been Helena's greatest friend in the family, all their differences were instantly forgotten as she journeyed to Cumberland House so she could offer her support to the grieving mother and clasp her in her arms. Five years earlier, Alix had also known the grief of losing a son, when her sixth and youngest child, Alexander John, had only lived for twenty-four hours. A memorial window for Harald was made by the Royal Windsor Stained Glass Works and placed in the Royal Chapel.

Twelve months later, an unnamed stillborn son on 7 May 1877 would be the sixth and last of their children. Queen Victoria was at Windsor when she received a telegram just after 1.00 p.m. to say that Helena had been taken ill. When she arrived at Cumberland Lodge she found Christian and the household very concerned. After a severe confinement, the baby was born early in the evening.

The Queen noted in her journal:

> Poor Lenchen kept asking if it was alive, which I much feared it would not be. Alas! Alas! it had never breathed. Too sad, & such a splendid child. After last year, for this to happen, is too tragic. I cannot help feeling that all was not done which should have been. It was such a splendid child & it was too piteous to see it lying there dead. Poor dear Lenchen was very exhausted by her long drawn out sufferings & naturally broken hearted at the loss of her Baby, but she was very brave & good. Christian was terribly upset...Left...carrying away with me a very sad recollection of what had occurred, but very grateful to God for having spared my

dear Child, & that I had been able to be there to comfort & support her & poor Christian.[28]

Louise later commissioned the French sculptor Aimee-Jules Dalou to produce a memorial to the two youngest who had been taken all too soon. Working in his Chelsea studio, he produced a poignant design showing an angel with two small children.

Despite her steely exterior, Helena was a prey to bouts of severe depression, exacerbated after the loss of her two youngest sons. She knew better than to try and confide in her mother on such an issue, and it is probable that the only two people who were sympathetic enough and prepared to understand were her devoted husband and her eldest sister. By the time she was forty the German Crown Princess had also experienced the deep sorrow of losing her two youngest sons. While she had at least been spared the birth of a stillborn child, her fourth son Waldemar was a particularly delightful child whose death from diphtheria at the age of eleven was a family tragedy from which she never really recovered. Such a shared experience doubtless helped to draw both sisters closer together in middle age.

- 4 -

'The want of truthfulness & openness' 1877-90

As the children became older, with more time on her hands Helena devoted more and more time to the charities, of which she was such an active patron. In her outlook and ideas she was close to her sister Alice in Germany, although as a minor princess she would never be able to exercise such authority. She began close to home, setting up a holiday house for deprived and handicapped children near Cumberland Lodge, which she supervised herself when she could. Nursing was and always remained a cause dear to her heart, and she made a careful study of English, French and German hospitals. She was a founder member of the Red Cross, and her work later attracted the admiration of Florence Nightingale. Marie Louise would later recall her sister and herself being set to work at rolling bandages to be used for the wounded during the Russo-Turkish War of 1877-8.

For a while, there was every chance that Britain could be drawn into war on behalf of Turkey against Russia, a conflict which would have had severe repercussions for the royal family. Helena's favourite brother Alfred, Duke of Edinburgh, had married Grand Duchess Marie of Russia, daughter of Tsar Alexander II, in 1874. He could thus have found himself in the unenviable position of being a senior naval commander engaged in action against his wife's country. Although Britain did manage to stand aside, the Duke was inadvertently involved in one embarrassing episode when he invited Prince Alexander of Battenberg, who was serving in the Russian navy, on board his ship in the Mediterranean for a brief fraternal reunion with his elder brother Louis, who was serving under the Duke. When news reached England, the Admiralty were horrified, and Queen Victoria was furious, with his foolishness which in some eyes was verging on treason. Even Helena wrote to one or two members of the family to admit that she was ashamed of being his sister. Alexander was horrified at being the unintentional cause of such a furore.[1] At length it was established that no harm had been done, and the unpleasantness proved only of short duration.

Despite her childhood lack of interest in sewing and embroidery – which had clearly been a phase that did not last - she also became founding President of the Royal School of Needlework, which had been founded in 1872 by Lady Victoria Welby. Established as the School of Art Needlework, it was set up partly to revive a form of art which was in danger of becoming lost, and through its revival, to provide employment for women who would otherwise be without means of a suitable livelihood. It was helped in its early days by William Morris and some of his friends and colleagues in the Arts and Crafts movement, and it received its royal prefix in March 1875 when Queen Victoria consented to become its first patron.

At committee meetings for her charities, Helena took charge and conducted the proceedings with a brisk, businesslike, even authoritarian spirit. When a proposal was made or suggested with which she concurred, it was noted, 'If anyone ventures to disagree with Her Royal Highness she has simply said, "It is my wish, that is sufficient," which always ended the discussion.'[2] Her niece Princess Alice, Countess of Athlone, recalled many years later a lady who was very kind and equable, and bore herself with great dignity, but would brook no contradiction. Once something had been discussed, it was a case of 'So we all agree on that point, don't we? Therefore, let us pass on...'[3] regardless of whether everybody had expressed agreement or not. One assumes that nobody dared to disagree.

It was characteristic of her no-nonsense personality, in which she was very much her mother's daughter. One Sunday, during a major dock strike, she and her family attended a church service at which a special prayer of intercession for settlement of the dispute, written by the Archbishop of Canterbury, was to be said. She picked up a copy, scrutinised it carefully through her glasses, and in what was described as the penetrating Royal Family whisper, remarked, 'That prayer won't settle any strike,' as she put it down. The passage which provoked her scorn was apparently a rather long-winded one inviting everyone to pray for 'a fuller realisation of our brotherhood'.[4]

No needy case was too small or insignificant to attract her attention. When her son told her of a local institute for the welfare of soldiers in Aldershot which had accumulated considerable debts, she arranged a charity concert, featuring several well-known names. Keen to help the unemployed, the poorer residents of the borough and their children, Helena hosted a programme of free dinners for them at the Guildhall at Windsor. She presided over two such occasions, in February and March 1886, and during the bitter winter that year over three thousand meals were served to the needy. Her efforts were recognized, and it was said that the poor of Windsor positively 'worshipped her'. It went on to become a regular fixture for some years every January. Early in 1888 clergymen and ladies joined in helping to serve a meal of soup, bread and rice pudding to a large group of children, with the promise that this would continue twice a week during the winter season. Three months later she was particularly touched when a ceremony was held at the Albert Institute, Windsor, at which she was presented with a diamond and sapphire pendant and diamond ring, subscribed for by the people of the town and district in recognition of her work. Accompanied by an album containing the names of the subscribers, both items had been produced at a cost of £600.

In 1879 the Order of St John of Jerusalem established a network of centres throughout the country, in which volunteers undertook instruction in administering first aid. Helena founded one centre in Windsor, and became President. She was punctilious in attending lectures, and accordingly went on to take and pass several examinations, as a result of which she was awarded the medallion of the Order. Later she regularly presented certificates and medallions to other successful candidates on completion of their courses and examinations. In 1882 she translated Professor Friedrich von Esmarch's *First Aid to the Injured* into English. She also contributed a preface, in which she wrote:

> The satisfaction of being able to tender the needed aid to those in pain, and of possibly being the means of saving a valued life, should more than counterbalance the scruples that some might feel on entering such a study.[5]

Life at Cumberland Lodge was very comfortable. The Christians' generally untroubled existence revolved largely around leisure pursuits, attendance on the Queen, public duties and their philanthropic activities. The children enjoyed having the freedom of the park, with plenty of space to ride, play, and go fishing or shooting. Christian Victor was taught by one of the footmen how to play cricket when he was aged about six, and he became passionate about the game, playing it at home, at school, university, and later on army service abroad. Albert also took it up when he was old enough to do so.

Queen Victoria took it upon herself to pay for several members of their staff, including a housekeeper and two housemaids. She helped Helena to decide on the livery for their servants. However there were limits to Her Majesty's munificence. In the summer of 1874, when Christian made numerous requests for such facilities as a telegraph, thirteen new coach houses, a laundry and dairy, all with rooms above for servants, she only allowed the first of these. It was necessary to remind him, she declared, that all outlay on Royal Residences placed her and the whole royal; family 'in a very invidious and disagreeable position'. As £10,000 had recently been spent on refurbishing Cumberland Lodge, there was 'nothing more likely to wake the attention of the House of Commons.'[6] She had evidently been less indifferent to recent republican mutterings in the country than might have been supposed. However, less than two years later she agreed to the provision of four more rooms on the upper floor of the house for family use. When the children came in covered in mud after walking or riding in the Park, they could reach these by the back stairs, as they were not allowed to go, or be seen, on the main staircase unless they were neat and tidy.

According to the 1881 census, at Cumberland Lodge the live-in domestic staff included a housekeeper, a cook, four housemaids, a stillroom maid, a kitchen maid, a scullery-maid, an under-butler, three footmen, one under-footman, and a coal porter. Additional servants would visit the house every day for various duties. A footman testified to Helena's personal kindness, saying that she was like a mother to them. She immediately noticed if anybody had a cold or was feeling unwell, and would send them to her dresser for some suitable remedy.[7] She always had an easy manner with servants and new ladies-in-waiting as she initiated them into their duties.

Helena and Christian spent some time with the Queen almost every day. They were either in attendance at a function, or else keeping her company while she was at home. In turn she regularly visited them at Cumberland Lodge, generally calling in to see the children while she was driving in the Park. They were also with her much of the time on their regular visits to Osborne and Balmoral.

Helena was devoted to members of her husband's family, and particularly pleased when it became apparent that there would be another marriage alliance between one of his nieces and her eldest nephew. Prince William of Prussia had become very attached to Princesses Augusta Victoria (Dona) and Caroline Matilda (Calma), the daughters of Christian's elder brother Frederick, the dispossessed Duke of Schleswig-Holstein. It soon became apparent that Dona was the one to whom the future German

Emperor had lost his heart. During his courtship of her in the summer of 1878, noted the Crown Princess, he seemed to be writing 'more expansively to his aunt [Helena] than to me'.[8] In September 1879 Dona told Helena that she would 'do all in her power to be a comfort' to the Crown Princess in order to show her gratitude for the 'great love and kindness' shown by the woman who would probably become her mother-in-law.[9]

William and Dona became engaged in January 1880, but a formal announcement was delayed by the illness and death later that month of Duke Frederick. After his funeral, both of his daughters came to England in order to spend some time at Cumberland Lodge, arriving on 14 February and staying for three weeks. The news of their betrothal could not be made public while the family were in mourning, and William also spent a month with his uncle and aunt.

Several of the family went to Berlin for the wedding of the future German Emperor and Empress in February 1881, arriving at different times. Among the guests were Helena and Christian. When the Prince of Wales stepped off the train in the Berlin capital, he was welcomed by a party of officers in Prussian army uniform. As he caught sight of a familiar face, he quietly asked one of his equerries the name of 'that old German general', whom he was sure he had seen before. The man informed him that it was His Royal Highness Prince Christian, his brother-in-law.

In November 1881, nine months after the young couple were married and when she was expecting their first child, it was to Helena that William turned to ask if she could help to find a nurse for the baby when born. Although it was common knowledge that relations were strained between the German prince and his mother, the family were astonished. The German Crown Princess was extremely hurt, although she begged Queen Victoria not to say anything about it to Helena, 'as she is most kind and of course cannot help it if Willie wishes to consult her instead of me.'[10] The shocked Queen advised Helena to have nothing to do with the request, as it was thoroughly tactless of William to have approached his aunt on such a subject without consulting his mother first.

At one stage, it had looked as if there might be another marriage alliance between the families. Now in his late twenties, Helena's youngest brother Leopold was looking for a bride. However, as he was known to be a haemophiliac who bruised easily and had often given the family cause for alarm, he was never going to be regarded as a particularly eligible husband. When he had met Calma he liked her very much and hoped to be able to propose to her one day. But Helena hinted that her niece was subject to 'nervous attacks', and that with health problems on both sides, for that reason alone a marriage between them was inadvisable. Anxious not to let a potentially suitable bride for her youngest son slip by, as he had had so many disappointments in life, Queen Victoria wanted one of her doctors to investigate the matter. If this was true, she said, then Calma should probably reconcile herself to not marrying at all. Believing her daughter might be to blame, she told Vicky that the difficulty was 'the want of truthfulness & openness in Lenchen who governs Christian entirely.'[11]

Marie, Duchess of Edinburgh, the wife of Helena's favourite brother Alfred, also distrusted the role that Helena and Christian were playing. Later the family were informed that Duke Frederick had written a letter not long before his death in which he had expressly forbidden his daughter to considering a marriage with Leopold because of his condition, but as the latter had suspected that the marriage question did not become serious until after the Duke's death, he was sure it must be a ruse to keep the young couple apart simply because of his poor health. Like his mother and sister-in-law he resented the fact that Helena and Christian were probably being dishonest with him, and for a while there was a breach between them. Ironically, some years later Leopold's only son Charles, destined to become the last Duke of Saxe-Coburg Gotha, would become the husband of Calma's elder daughter.

Fortunately, for Leopold there was to be a happy conclusion to the business. Whatever the role Helena and Christian may or may not have played in the romance between Leopold and Calma, they were as pleased as the rest of the family in 1882 when her youngest brother proposed to and married Princess Helen of Waldeck-Pyrmont. Sadly but not surprisingly, his life of married bliss was destined to be cut short. In February 1884 he was advised to spend some time in Cannes, alone, for health reasons, leaving a pregnant Helen behind. At the end of March he slipped on a tiled floor, hit his knee, and died from a haemorrhage. Helena was visiting Helen at Claremont when she was handed a telegram containing the tragic news, which she had to break to the young widow.

At around this time Helena was involved in helping to prepare an edition of the letters of her late sister Alice, Grand Duchess of Hesse, to the Queen. This venture had a rather interesting origin. In 1883 a German publisher, Dr Arnold Bergsträsser, published a German translation of selections from the correspondence between mother and daughter, and subsequently received several offers from British publishers to bring out a translation. The German edition was prefaced with a biographical sketch by Dr Karl Sell, a clergyman in Darmstadt, who also introduced the letters and added some detailed comments. The situation was an ambiguous one, as the Queen had made the letters available to Sell. It was probable that she had allowed him to see them for research purposes, but she subsequently maintained that she had not given permission for their publication and was presumably expecting that her permission would be sought first had he wished to publish any of them. However, when the volume was available, Helena contacted Sell to ask him for permission to translate his text into English. Without consulting Bergsträsser, Sell readily gave permission, perhaps feeling that he was not in a position to refuse as her mother had copies of the associated letters anyway. Helena accordingly began to translate the material.

However, in December 1883 Bergsträsser claimed ownership of the copyright to the collection of the letters, and was requesting a delay in the publication of any English translation. Helena wrote to Sir Theodore Martin, who had recently completed publication of his officially authorised five-volume biography of the Prince Consort, to ask if he could help to clarify the position. Martin accordingly agreed to meet her, and she asked him if he would act informally as an intermediary to resolve the situation in a manner which would be satisfactory to all parties, culminating in the publication of the letters with Sell's text in English. Simultaneously she also asked Hermann Sahl, the royal librarian who had connections in Darmstadt, to act as another intermediary. Bergsträsser subsequently wrote to Martin, telling him that he was informed Princess Helena wished 'to regulate the matter of the book' through him, that he had received several offers from English publishers, and that the eventual publisher of the English edition could expect a generous fee. He was willing to travel to London and would very much like a personal interview with Martin on the matter. At length he was persuaded to abandon his efforts to delay publication of the English edition, and to modify his copyright claim in return for a suitable financial settlement.

In January 1884 he came to London to meet Martin and discuss royalty terms. Meanwhile Helena was insisting on behalf of the Queen that the copyright in the letters rested with the Queen, and that only the text by Sell was open to negotiation. Mother and daughter considered that Bergsträsser's demands were exorbitant and totally unjustified, and refused to communicate with him directly. After some negotiation, Bergsträsser was persuaded to withdraw his demand for a delay in publishing, and modify his copyright claims in return for a lump sum. He declared that he was willing to accept £100 for the first 3000 copies and a further £40 for each subsequent thousand copies sold. Once agreement was reached, Martin chose the publisher John Murray to issue the book.

In April 1884, with some assistance from Emily Loch's sister Alice, Helena wrote a preface to the volume, which was published that summer. In it, she noted that she felt confident that

> the perusal of these letters must deepen the love and admiration which has always been felt for my beloved Sister in this country, where she ever thanked God that her childhood and youth had been tended with a wise love, that had fostered and developed all those qualities and tastes which she most valued and strove to cultivate in her later years.[12]

Queen Victoria was naturally very impressed with the work, saying to the Crown Princess that Lenchen had 'done it with great refinement and feeling.'[13] It was well received by the public and sold out almost immediately.

Nevertheless, mother and daughter both found Bergsträsser's intervention totally unwarranted, and Helena regretted that he would doubtless 'receive far more than he is really at all entitled to',[14] on the grounds that the copyright actually belonged to the Queen as the letters were addressed to her, and that only Sell's original preface was open to negotiation. In 1885 a 'new and popular edition' was published. This time John Murray removed Sell's text and substituted a 53-page memoir written by Helena. The problem of paying any royalties to Sell was thus avoided, and the fact that Helena gave her name to the memoir to her sister attracted greater interest in the book.

In March 1887, Helena and Christian went to Berlin to represent Queen Victoria at celebrations to mark the ninetieth birthday of Emperor William. Their gift to him was a large steel engraving of the battle of Rorke's Drift. While they were there, Helena was apparently party to one or two interesting conversations with the German Crown Princess and Crown Prince Rudolf of Austria-Hungary. At the time there were fears that war might break out between Austria and Russia over territorial disputes in the Balkans, where the situation had been delicate ever since Prince Alexander of Battenberg had been forced by Russian troops to abdicate his position as sovereign Prince of Bulgaria the previous autumn.

How much or how little Helena was involved is open to question. Knowing that her eldest sister was very unpopular with the ruling party in Berlin, it seems unlikely that she would have taken any active part in any discussions, and would more likely have been there as simply a close observer of matters concerning members of the family – but nothing more. Like her mother and siblings she was known to be a champion of 'poor Sandro', the recently deposed prince of Bulgaria, although she tended to be discreet in her opinions. She was aware that Emperor William and Bismarck, like Tsar Alexander III of Russia, were extremely hostile to him, and that any words or gestures of support for him would only inflame he matter.

According to reports written afterwards by her nephew Prince William, the future Emperor, Crown Prince Rudolf told him that he thought Princess Christian was 'a highly intelligent, clever lady, but quite definitely an intriguer', who 'spoke most in the conversation whenever the Crown Princess slowed down a little.' William later commented to Herbert Bismarck, son of the German Chancellor, that he made efforts to persuade Rudolf that Queen Victoria was trying to use her daughters as agents in order to increase British influence in the Balkans, perhaps by persuading the Austrian government to bring pressure to bear on Russia, or maybe even threaten war, in reinstating Alexander as Prince of Bulgaria. The Prince of Wales, William went on, was 'not discreet enough for such delicate matters, which is why he has not been given a clear mission, and his sisters have told him to hold his tongue and not mess up his work for them.'[15] Rudolf, who liked and admired the German Crown Prince and Princess and shared their liberal views, disliked William, whose distrust of his English relatives was well-known, and it is highly likely that the latter was deliberately putting words into the Austrian heir's mouth. The Prussian Minister of Agriculture Lucius von Balhausen, a colleague and admirer of the Bismarcks, later noted in his diary that Chancellor Bismarck 'was quite furious at the Frau Crown Princess and the Princess Christian, who had taken the Crown Prince of Austria between them and tried to convince him that Austria must reinstate the Battenberger in Bulgaria and make him the ruler there even against Russia's will.'[16] As one of the most virulently Anglophobe politicians in Berlin and a bitter enemy of the German Crown Princess, his words can hardly be taken at face value. (In his memoirs, Balhausen would later state that the following year a heartless Empress Victoria left her ailing husband one day to go for a walk and came back to find him dead).

That Helena would have ever tried to take it on herself to try and act as an agent in such matters, let alone tell her elder brother to 'hold his tongue', is difficult to believe. She would have been far too sensible to try and interfere in anything which was not her business, and also well aware that to do so would reflect badly on her and on the family. From reading her nephew's dispatches, it is hard to avoid the conclusion that the hot-headed young man was deliberately spreading gossip in order to blacken members of his mother's family. He had generally been close to his aunt and uncle, but even so he was not inclined to spare them any more than the others in his efforts to make mischief – and it is hard to explain his motives otherwise.

At around this time, Helena made two further ventures into the world of publication. She was engaged in translating from the French and writing an introduction to a new edition of the memoirs of Wilhelmina, Margravine of Bayreuth, sister of Frederick the Great. Much of her research was carried out in person in the Royal Library at Berlin, possibly with some assistance from her late father's former librarian Ruland.

In her introduction, she explained that certain 'suppressions' were necessary, and entirely justified by the 'coarse character of the original'. She also wrote about the characters of the King and his sister in terms which, given her royal blood, show a remarkable insight into radical thought. The Margravine, she wrote, was a woman who stood out 'in marked prominence among the most gifted women' of her age, through her kindness, self-sacrificing devotion, and friendship with others. Even more significantly, she and her brother, Helena wrote, were among the first of 'those questioning minds that strove after spiritual freedom', in having studied the works of the English and French philosophers. In the eighteenth century, she observed, 'began the great struggle of philosophy and French tyranny and worn out abuses which culminated in the French revolution', a struggle in which 'the noblest minds were engaged'.[17]

During the late nineteenth century, a royal generation, that of Queen Victoria, her contemporary Empress Augusta of Germany, and others, looked on the French revolution as a subject not fit for discussion. The Queen's daughters were generally of a more enquiring mind, and were fearless in risking the disapproval of others in their readiness to take an interest in the writings of the free thinkers of their day. Crown Princess Frederick William was sufficiently curious about socialism to obtain a copy of Karl Marx's *Das Kapital* and, having read it, to ask a friend, the Member of Parliament Sir M.E. Grant Duff, to visit Marx in England (where he had settled after his expulsion from Prussia) and send her a report on his impressions of the man. Marx, he noted, mentioned the Crown Prince and Princess several times and spoke of them 'invariably with due respect and propriety', something which was not reserved for other eminent individuals.[18] Alice had shocked certain members of royalty, particularly the German Empress, because of her friendship with the controversial theologian David Friedrich Strauss, while Louise was noted for her unconventional views and Bohemian tendencies. Like them, Helena refused to accept the status quo and was determined to make her own mind up on such matters.

The book was published by David Stott in September 1887, and generally well received. In its review, *The Times* praised it warmly, acknowledging that in view of the circulation of court scandals 'in undignified coarseness', a reflection of a less refined age, the Princess had 'exercised a wise discretion in suppressing some of the more questionable passages, though we confess to having no great fancy for Bowdlerized editions'.[19] According to the *Saturday Review*, the translation was 'sound, and it has the higher accuracy of spirit.'[17] Eight months later the same publisher issued *The Margravine of Bayreuth and Voltaire*, a volume of letters covering the years 1742 to 1758, edited with explanatory notes by a Berlin scholar, Dr Georg Horn. Again, Helena was responsible for the translation of the material.

By this time Helena's regular visits abroad during the late summer and early autumn were well established. She was regularly to be seen at European health spas, especially Wiesbaden, Homburg and Nauheim, where the effect of the waters was thought to be beneficial. They were highly charged with various minerals, thought to be good for health, and from the eighteenth century, entrepreneurs and authorities alike exploited the medicinal benefits to attract large numbers of people. Doctors would also descend on the resorts, and additional attractions such as meeting places, assembly rooms, concerts, entertainments and casinos were provided. These breaks were undertaken not merely for her own good, but also partly as a holiday, a break from the routine of life at home. For a short time she and other royalties, notably the Prince of Wales, could relax with and pay visits to friends, listen to music, and maybe even try their hand at the gambling tables. Christian very rarely accompanied her, but she generally took Helena Victoria and Marie Louise with her, ensuring that they took advantage of the ample opportunities to visit family, concerts and the opera.

For Helena, an additional reason for coming here was because they would be near Darmstadt, and she could thus pay regular visits to her motherless nephew and nieces. Since her elder sister, their mother Alice, had succumbed to diphtheria in December 1878, leaving four daughters and a son aged between fifteen and six, Queen Victoria and her children went out of their way to keep a close eye on them and their widowed father Louis, Grand Duke of Hesse.

Helena's perpetual unsatisfactory health was particularly acute at this time, and caused the family some anxiety. Her illness was never exactly defined, although it has been suggested that much of her physical pain was caused by neuralgia, 'a fashionable and non-specific complaint of the time'.[20] While at Windsor she was regularly consulting different doctors, whose solution, it appears, was to prescribe her various 'cures' which failed to work. At least one stay at Homburg failed to prove immediately efficacious. When they arrived in September 1886, Christian for once accompanying her on this occasion, she was clearly unwell. Two days into their sojourn, she took to her bed immediately after dinner with a particularly bad neuralgic attack. Three days later, a concerned Emily Loch noted, she seemed better before dinner 'but was dreadfully bad all evening with neuralgia and everyone was in despair'.[21]

In 1887, shortly after the busy summer of the Queen's jubilee celebrations in London, Helena and Emily were in Wiesbaden. Her health was still giving cause for concern and in addition she was worried about her eyesight, fearing at one stage that she might be going blind. They consulted Dr Herman Pagenstecher, an eminent German ophthalmologist and head of the Wiesbaden Eye Clinic, who was also based for a while at the London Eye Hospital. Whether Helena suffered from glaucoma or cataract, or some other condition entirely, is unclear. The treatments she underwent involved having caustic put in her eye, and 'the eyelid being turned inside out and burned'.

After discussing her case with Dr James Reid, Queen Victoria's physician, Pagenstecher decided that she had been exaggerating her complaints. There was nothing wrong with her eyes, he maintained, and her symptoms were 'simply the result of her nerves being for the time shattered by stimulants and narcotics and ceased when these were for the time being cut from her'. Although Emily Loch is non-judgemental and fairly discreet on the subject, she hinted that the Princess was in considerably better health when not attending clinics and being examined by doctors, and when she had better things, or more fulfilling activities, to fill her time.[22]

Helena evidently had great faith in Pagenstecher. In 1888 she returned to Germany to seek his advice again, and later she asked him if he would come to Osborne so he could treat her mother when her sight was failing during her last years. However, the treatment she underwent goes at least part of the way to explain what has often been described superficially as her 'drug addiction', a rather melodramatic term. Cocaine was used extensively by the medical profession at that time as a local anaesthetic, and in the case of eye treatment, for expanding the pupil during operations. Laudanum, a tincture of opium, was a standard Victorian ingredient in pain relief. As Prime Minister, Gladstone was regularly said to have taken some in his coffee prior to appearing before the House of Commons, while Charles Dickens sometimes used it to help him sleep and to steady his nerves. In the nineteenth century, such drugs were the equivalent of today's over-the-counter painkillers. The perils of over-reliance, even addiction, of such substances, were not fully appreciated at the time. Had her doctors not treated her with them so heavily, Helena's health might not have been affected so much. As the drugs were eventually discontinued, and she went on to enjoy a relatively fit and active old age, she was fortunate in not suffering any permanent harm from them.

One of the charities with which she became involved at around this time, and would work hard for over the next few years, was the British Nurses' Association. In 1887 she was chosen to become President on its foundation by her friend Mrs Bedford Fenwick. In her acceptance speech she said that the first object of the Association was to obtain for the calling of nursing the recognised position and legal constitution of a profession. 'It will follow from this that in future every member of the nursing profession must have been educated up to a definite standard of knowledge and efficiency.'[23] Over the next few years, she attended regular meetings in London in this capacity. She also designed a badge for the Association, in which she incorporated the motto so beloved by her father, 'Steadfast and true'.

Always ready to champion worthy causes in the press, in July 1888 she published a letter in *The Times*. This gave her a platform to draw attention to the fact that there were now 15,000 trained nurses in Britain, and that this was largely due to the experiences of the Crimean War, and the noble efforts of Florence Nightingale who had worked so valiantly by exposing the shocking lack of nursing facilities available in time of conflict. 'No surgeon or physician,' she wrote, 'would willingly take charge of a serious case without the assistance of a trained nurse, and the medical profession as a body has borne the most prompt and generous testimony to the great value of skilled nursing.'[24]

The year 1888 also saw one of the great family tragedies which was to have a major impact on the course of European history during the next thirty years. All of Queen Victoria's children had eagerly looked forward to the day when the eldest of them would be Empress Consort in Berlin, and her husband would reign as Emperor Frederick III. By the time his nonagenarian father Emperor William died in March, Frederick was a dying man himself. Fatally stricken with cancer of the larynx, by the time of his accession he was unable to speak above a hoarse whisper. He too went to the grave in June, aged fifty-six, after a reign of ninety-nine days. Sir Morell Mackenzie, the British doctor who had been in charge of the case, was strongly condemned by his German counterparts for alleged mismanagement of his patient's illness. Within a month of his death they had published a pamphlet attacking him, to which he responded with his own defensive diatribe in book form three months later. Even in Britain, he had few defenders, with medical colleagues accusing him of having violated the secrets of the sickroom. The Royal College of Surgeons in London proposed to bring up a resolution concerning his book and censuring him.

Helena also made efforts to intercede on her elder sister's behalf and, noted Dr Reid, 'opened fire' on him on behalf of the Empress, who was staying in England at the time. She was evidently attempting to bring pressure to bear on the royal doctors, namely Reid and the Queen's Sergeant Surgeon, Sir James Paget, to try and dissuade the Council from pursuing the issue so publicly. Reid advised Paget that in his view, Princess Christian was 'not a very satisfactory person to understand reason or logic,' and he made it clear to her that the Council could not 'evade its duty.'[25] Mackenzie, it seemed to them, was increasingly becoming a rather divisive character in the medical profession, disliked and distrusted by his colleagues and therefore a liability. Now he was trying to involve the Queen in the controversy surrounding the late Emperor's treatment, and suggesting that she was endorsing everything he had done with regard to the case. Now she regretted that the 'Mackenzie affair' was continuing to cause annoyance, and she was adamant that her name should not be used or facts misrepresented in any manner. In the end Mackenzie was persuaded to resign his membership of the Royal College of Physicians, and the case was not formally discussed.

Like Arthur, Duke of Connaught, Helena had always been on much better terms with their nephew William, now Emperor, than the rest of their siblings. Yet this did not prevent the widowed Empress Frederick from becoming much closer to her sister throughout the rest of her life. Helena spent some time in Germany during the early weeks of her sister's widowhood, comforting her, and reported to Lady Ponsonby (4 August 1888) that she had never seen 'such a courageous woman – for crushed and broken-hearted under a load of sorrow and care such as few have ever had to bear, she always pulls herself together.' At times Helena confessed that it was all she could do to keep her tears back when she looked at her sister's face 'with that expression of mental pain and suffering on it.'

She was also a valuable help in the matter of helping to sort out much of her sister's private correspondence. Just over a year earlier, when they left for England to go and take part in Queen Victoria's jubilee celebrations, Crown Prince Frederick William had taken several boxes of private papers for safe keeping at Windsor Castle, as they both feared that such documents would not be safe in Germany after his death. Heinrich von Friedberg, the German minister of justice, told the Empress that the Emperor, Bismarck and the ministers of state were demanding that they be returned, as they were German state property. He reassured her by promising that he would examine them in her presence, so that he could vouch for the fact that they consisted of purely private papers and could argue the case for this to the Emperor and others. The boxes therefore came with Helena's luggage and arrived at Potsdam on 19 July. Friedberg was as good as his word, and duly confirmed that as they were private papers, the ministry had no claim on them.

Helena undertook the sad task of sorting through them with her sister. Some of them were returned to the writers, while those to Queen Victoria and the Prince Consort were sent back to the British Embassy for eventual safe keeping once again at Windsor, and others, mainly those the Empress had received from her brothers, sisters and close friends, were '*burnt*, with a heavy heart'.[26]

As for the general conduct of her nephew, now Emperor, Helena was able to report to Lady Ponsonby that

> so far he has been very nice and pleasant with his mother, but of course he <u>does</u> do a thousand and one things which hurt and pain her, and which one would give worlds he did <u>not</u> do. But I really think he does them out of thoughtlessness and certainly not from premeditation. I have said and done my very utmost to try and smooth down matters and have implored her to take him as much into her confidence as she can by consulting him about trifles. This would flatter and please him – and she would unconsciously gain a far greater influence than she at present has any idea of....I am so thankful I have been with her, and she makes me so happy by saying that I am a comfort and help – would that I <u>could</u> do <u>anything</u> to lighten her burden![27]

Helena knew that she was better placed than anybody else in the family to try and repair relations between mother and son at such a tragic time. The Empress had already told her sister that it was no use pandering to his tyranny and playing up to his little foibles, as her mother-in-law, Dowager Empress Augusta, had shamelessly done. Nevertheless Helena was in the almost unique position of being able to see matters from both sides. In the years to come, the Empress would understand her eldest son a little better and go some way towards forgiving him, while she could never forget how much he had hurt her.

Such efforts may have taken their toll on Helena. In September she returned to Wiesbaden, but had to see a doctor almost every day. On 28 September she was in bed all day suffering from neuralgia, and for about a month from 11 October onwards she was either in bed or else confined to her room. For much of that time she also had a night nurse in attendance. Not until the third week of November was she well enough to return to England.

Throughout the year of 1889 she spent much of her time in Germany. During the spring she and her daughters were at Wiesbaden, when they passed most of their days and evenings paying visits to friends and to the theatre, or else spending quiet hours at their hotel playing card games or writing letters. That autumn, while they were at Frankfurt, they attended a number of concerts. One of particular interest was given in aid of the Red Cross and held at the Casino, and featured music that had been written by Frederick the Great, a gifted flautist as well as composer, and his nephew Prince Louis Ferdinand of Prussia.

While Helena was one of those who helped to pave the way for a gradual if perhaps never complete reconciliation between the Empress Frederick and her eldest son, there were still occasions when she would be caught in the middle of the crossfire. After Vicky's third daughter Sophie married Constantine, Crown Prince of the Hellenes, in October 1889, she announced to the family that as a future Queen consort of the country, she intended to enter the Orthodox Church. As head of the family, Emperor William was furious that his sister should take such a step without consulting him, seemingly disregarding or at any rate taking little account of the fact that she had married into another dynasty altogether. He and the then heavily pregnant Empress Augusts Victoria rebuked her severely, and a major quarrel developed. He was so incensed that he threatened to forbid her from entering Germany again as long as she lived, a 'life sentence' which he later reduced to three years.

The quarrel sooner or later involved several other members of the family, and the Emperor seemed sure he would find a ready ally in his aunt Helena. She was alleged to have told the Empress's Lord Chamberlain, Baron Hugo von Reischach, that the Empress had 'ill-treated William until he cried!"[28] It seems most unlikely that the level-headed Helena would have ever believed such an assertion, but she clearly did not relish having to be involved in such petty squabbles.

During the next few years she would be a regular visitor to Germany each summer and autumn, coming to the spa at Bad Homburg, and on several occasions she would stay with her sister. Vicky was always on hand with sympathy, ready to help her younger sister in the slow but ultimately successful business of weaning her off the drugs, and the bond between them became ever stronger. During what had become a more or less annual visit to the spa at Wiesbaden, she and her daughters spent several weeks in Berlin with the Empress Frederick and her family, prior to the wedding of the Empress's second daughter, another Victoria ('Moretta'), to Prince Adolf of Schaumburg-Lippe, in November 1890. Helena and Christian were also treated to regular hospitality from the Emperor and Empress, who were very fond of their aunt and uncle despite their differences with so many of their other relations in England, and often went out of their way to impress them.

At the time it seemed to most if not all of the guests that the bride's happiness was assured, after she was forbidden to marry the dashing but unfortunate Alexander of Battenberg, whose reign as Sovereign Prince of Bulgaria had ended in enforced abdication and exile. Nevertheless the marriage had been largely arranged by her eldest brother, the Emperor. It would endure until Adolf's death in 1916, though it was perhaps not the most successful of unions and the couple never had any children.

Helena and Christian left Germany for England shortly before Christmas. By then they knew that there would soon be another wedding to plan, and one in which they would be more closely involved than the others.

- 5 -

'Violent opinions and very often absurd tirades' 1891-1900

The children of Helena and Christian were now approaching a marriageable age. It was therefore sad that only one of them did go to the altar, and even more so that that union was destined to end in divorce, with no children, within less than a decade. On the family's visit to Berlin in November 1890 to attend the wedding of Princess Victoria of Prussia to Prince Adolf of Schaumburg-Lippe, Helena and Christian were told that Prince Ferdinand of Roumania, heir to his childless uncle King Carol, was interested in the possibility of Marie Louise as a possible bride. However she was not attracted to him, partly as she was more taken by another suitor for her hand, Prince Aribert of Anhalt.

Always happy to see his cousins marrying good German princes, Emperor William promised to help smooth their path, and the young couple were subsequently engaged at a family party in Potsdam. Writing to Emily Baird (formerly Emily Maude) to thank her for her good wishes on her daughter's engagement, Helena said that the prospect of the forthcoming marriage 'makes us very happy, as we feel that with God's blessing a very happy future is in store for her.'[1] They were however obliged to ask the Emperor for financial support to help provide the couple with enough money to live on, a request to which he generously agreed. Under the circumstances, Queen Victoria was obliged to invite him to the wedding, something which she had not originally planned to do.

In the summer of 1891 Helena and Christian celebrated their silver wedding anniversary at Windsor, with Christian Victor travelling five thousand miles from India to return home and join them for the occasion.

On 3 July they were presented with various addresses and souvenirs, including a service of silver plate, at a special ceremony held at the Town Hall by the Mayor and Corporation. It was a time of double festivities, for three days later Marie Louise and Aribert were married. The proud parents doubtless assumed that it would not be long before they attended the weddings of their other children, but in this they would ultimately be disappointed.

The elder daughter, Helena Victoria, who was increasingly becoming her parents' devoted companion, must have looked on with a sense of envy at seeing her younger sister becoming a bride. Helena herself was likewise a little saddened that at the age of thirty this daughter was still a spinster. Clever, hardworking, friendly and kindhearted if somewhat plain in looks, she would have made any prince a good steady wife. For a time it seemed there was the possibility that she would become betrothed to her cousin Prince Albert Victor (Eddy) of Wales, second in succession to the throne after his father, or to his younger brother George. However their mother's resentment of the family after the issue of the Schleswig-Holstein duchies nearly thirty years previously had created a lasting rift between the families. Outwardly a placid, charming woman, the Princess of Wales had never really forgiven 'the Christians', and she was thus implacably opposed to the mere idea of one of their daughters ever becoming her daughter-in-law.

Helena had hoped that there might be an engagement between them, and when Eddy was betrothed to Princess Victoria Mary (May) of Teck, daughter of Francis, Duke of Teck and the former Princess Mary of Cambridge, Queen Victoria was most distressed at Helena having been unpleasant to the family. She was not at all pleased, the Queen wrote to the Empress Frederick, '& does not unfortunately keep it to herself - & was (to my horror) positively rude to Mary & May...& both Mary & Alix were distressed at it (it made me so hot) & she has been imprudent enough to speak to other people abt. it, I can't understand it.'[2] Louise, Marchioness of Lorne, also looked on the engagement with some disfavour, and the Queen was convinced that both sisters were jealous of Mary's popularity.

Helena and Christian did not give up all hope. Eddy died in January 1892, a mere six weeks after his engagement, leaving his one surviving brother, the far more dependable George. The Princess of Wales was extremely scathing about Helena Victoria and her parents' aspirations that she might become engaged to the prince who was now second in line to the throne. 'So the Xtians have been following you about with their lovely Snipe! well it will be a pleasure to welcome that beauty as yr bride – when may we expect the news?'[3] she wrote sarcastically to her son. To her relief it was not to be, and George duly became engaged to May and they were married in July 1893.

The 'lovely Snipe', thus nicknamed because of her rather long nose, would remain a lifelong spinster. During the autumn of 1891 she and Prince Ernest, heir to the duchy of Hesse and the Rhine had been among the Queen's guests at Balmoral and some of the elder generation had briefly hoped that romance between both cousins might blossom, but it was not to be. At the wedding of George and May, created Duke and Duchess of York, Helena Victoria was one of the bridesmaids. It was however said that Helena had been less than pleased at her being invited to assume such a role, when it had at one time seemed possible that she might have been the bride at the wedding instead.

As far as Helena and Christian were concerned, it had been a difficult time for other reasons. On the afternoon of Boxing Day 1891 Christian went out with his son Albert, and his brothers-in-law the Duke of Connaught and Henry of Battenberg, to go shooting in the royal preserves at Osborne. One shot fired by the Duke glanced off the bough of a tree and hit Christian, with three pellets entering his face and one his left eye, and he was taken back to the house in great pain. Writing in her journal, the Queen, who 'was in despair & horrified,' noted that 'poor Lenchen is naturally in great distress, but was very courageous & calm..., I can't describe my distress for poor Lenchen & Christian, & for poor unfortunate Arthur'.[4]

George Lawson, the Queen's oculist, was summoned at once. After examining Christian's eye he said that there was unfortunately no possibility of saving it, and that there would be a risk of danger to the sight in the other if it was not removed immediately. But first Reid had to seek the Queen's permission to operate. Initially she declared firmly that to do so would be quite unnecessary, as she had known in the past of several people who had had similar injuries but did not have an eye removed and had not become blind as a result; 'nowadays doctors were always for taking out eyes; and in short she spoke as if Lawson and I wished to do it for our own brutal pleasure!'[5] At length she gave her consent, reluctantly, when he told her that Lawson would be quite willing to leave the eye, provided he was not to be blamed or held responsible, in the event of the Prince becoming blind. An operation was carried out next day under anaesthetic, with the assistance of Dr Reid and Dr Hoffmeister, the resident physician at Cowes.

At the time Christian Victor was serving with the army in India. In writing from Osborne (4 February 1892) to wish him a happy new year, the Queen sought to reassure him of the state of affairs at home:

...thank God! Dear Papa is as well as possible, taking quite long walks, looks very well and in good spirits. But oh! My dear child what an awful accident this has been in every way so distressing and tho he will not feel any real inconvenience and never had any pain or fever – the fact of the loss of an eye is a blemish for life – and a most painful thing. He has been so good and kind about it never grumbling or anything and only trying to prevent Uncle Arthur from being distressed. Mama has been wonderfully calm and patient after the first day.[6]

For Helena, it had indeed been a time of 'so much sorrow and anxiety lately,' as she wrote to Emily Baird (13 February 1892):

First my dear Husband's terrible anxiety, and then dear Eddy's death. It has been a terrible time. Christian is very well in health thank God, and made a very good recovery. You can understand what I went through and what I suffered. It was a dreadful time of anxiety. He has not really been out shooting but he went out for half an hour with his gun – as the oculist wanted him to try if he could see to shoot. He managed pretty well. He has been so wonderfully brave and patient all the time, and always cheerful.[7]

During the next few years Christian made a collection of glass eyes, including a bloodshot one that he said was for when he had a cold. He made light of his accident, and at parties at home he had a habit of removing one eye and replacing it with another, much to the discomfort of those present who were not used to his doing so. When he was on his own in the study, he would generally wear a pair of goggles with a green shield on one side and an open aperture on the other.[8]

Helena continued to find distraction from her troubles in her continued hard work on behalf of charities. From the beginning she had been keen to add the prefix 'Royal' to the British Nurses' Association, or RBNA. She wrote to Sir Henry Ponsonby (3 January 1891) to state their case.

The Association has been in existence 3 whole years – has done good work – is supported by all the leading Physicians and Surgeons of the country who aid us by their personal co-operation and advice. I fact, I may honestly say we are a most flourishing Institution in the face of much opposition and misrepresentation.

> If the Queen would grant the petition and become the Patron of the Association allowing it to call itself 'Royal British Nurses Ass[ociation] I and all concerned w[oul]d be so deeply grateful.[9]

She was a strong supporter of nurse registration, an issue supported by the Association on the grounds that it would protect the sick from the less expert ministrations of unskilled workers.

In 1892 the Association addressed a petition to the Queen for a Royal Charter of Incorporation to allow it to keep a register of qualified nurses, and the Privy Council heard the petition in November. Florence Nightingale and other leading public figures opposed it on the grounds that they believed it was too soon, and that registration and paper qualifications were inappropriate because of the personal qualities which were expected in a nurse. The decision of the Privy Council was given in May 1893, allowing the Charter and a list but not the word 'Register'. Nevertheless Helena was very gratified by such recognition. One week later, she was in Edinburgh at a meeting in the Synod Hall at which the Scottish National Branch of the Association was inaugurated.

In a speech which Helena made in 1893, she made clear that the RBNA was working towards improving the educational status of those devoted and self-sacrificing women whose whole lives have been devoted to tending the sick, the suffering, and the dying. At the same time she warned about the opposition and misrepresentation they had encountered. Although the RBNA was in favour of registration as a means of enhancing and guaranteeing the professional status of trained nurses, its incorporation with the Privy Council allowed it to maintain a list rather than a formal register of nurses. Taking the lead at the charitable bodies she represented as an active campaigner, she wrote letters to newspapers and magazines promoting the interests of registration. Her royal status helped to promote the publicity and society interest that surrounded such organisations. She also took a leading role in aiding the work of the Executive Committee in their determination to establish separate branches of the Association in Edinburgh and Dublin, so that members of the Association who lived in Scotland and Ireland 'should have some direct knowledge and be able to take a more direct and active part in the work' of the body.[10]

Another of her favourite charities, of which she had by this time long been an active President of the Royal School of Needlework, never content to be a mere figurehead. She would personally undertake such duties as writing to the Royal Commissioners to request funds, and in 1895, she asked for and was duly granted £30,000 towards erecting a building for the school in South Kensington. Her royal status aided in its promotion, and among the activities she took on its behalf were her Thursday afternoon tea parties at the school for society ladies, who were keen to be seen in the presence of members of the royal family. When its Christmas bazaars were held, she acted as chief saleswoman, generating long queues of people anxious to be served personally by her.

In May 1887 she had distributed the prizes at the annual exhibition of the prize schemes for needlework in the town hall at Oxford, at which ninety-one schools and 1,040 children had competed. Her speech, which as always came directly from the heart, testified to her love of the activity and her passion for it:

> I go so far as to think that every woman, in whatever sphere of life, should be taught to work and how to use her needle. I fear that there has been a great tendency to overlook the necessity of girls being taught good plain needlework... I know from personal experience the many pleasant hours I have spent in doing plain needlework and the pride I have felt when I had done some that was really good and useful.[11]

New charitable organisations were regularly being formed, and she eagerly supported these as well as becoming actively involved with several. One was the London Diocesan Council for Rescue and Prevention, founded in 1890. The welfare of prostitutes, and the betterment of girls driven by sheer poverty into such a way of life, was a matter in which there were some who would rather not be involved, but Helena would never be counted among that number. In December 1895 *The Times* published a letter from her in which she appealed for the formation of local associations in separate urban districts empowered to carry out such work, and for funds to enable them to carry it out. The aim of such bodies, she wrote, was 'to remove young girls from bad homes or perilous surroundings', and place them in training homes or 'carefully-chosen situations', and funds were needed to provide salaries to pay efficient workers, as well as finance temporary homes for girls who were brought under their care. 'I and those engaged in the work plead for the protection of young lives,' she concluded, 'for the restoration of the erring – our own sheltered homes plead silently for the cause. I cannot believe that we shall plead in vain.'[12]

In June 1896 she opened the Princess Christian Holiday Home for Boys, at Bishopsgate, Windsor Great Park. This institution could trace its origins in 1890, in response to an appeal made in the *Windsor and Eton Express* on behalf of the London Ragged School Union. A small house was found for the purpose in Bachelor's Acre, Windsor. During that summer and the one following, about 200 boys were given a fortnight's holiday at the home. On the expiry of the lease, as it was thought that a more complete country life would be better for them, a cottage in the grounds was rented. Each successive summer about 120 boys enjoyed, as she said in her opening address, 'the advantages of fresh air, recreation and good food, combined with the softening influence of a happy home life.'[13]

By 1895 the cottage was considered no longer fit for habitation, so she made herself responsible for the lease, as well as the building and furnishing of a cottage which would be fit for receiving a party of boys, with a married couple living there to take charge of them.

As ever, family activities continued to take up much of Helena's time. In the summer of 1892 she, her elder daughter Helena Victoria, and Emily Loch were all at Osborne during Cowes Week. The German Emperor was taking part in the regatta, and eagerly showing off his new yacht, although as ever he did not take too kindly if he was beaten in any of the races in which he took part. Yet he went out of his way to demonstrate his considerable charm to the family, and invited many of them on board to tea one afternoon. It was observed that he was paying particular attention to Helena, as the aunt whom he had long regarded as one of his greatest allies in England, and some of them were surprised to see him personally handing round teacakes and butter.

Helena was in the fortunate position of being on the best of terms with her nephew and her eldest sister. In her devotion to the latter, she took a particular interest in the activities and welfare of the younger Prussian princesses. Having attended the weddings of Sophie and Victoria, it was only natural that she should be invited to, and keen to attend, that of Margaret ('Mossy') to Prince Frederick Charles of Hesse in January 1893. As this took place in the depths of winter, it required a good deal of travel across Holland and Germany, both covered in snow, in a large saloon carriage 'with an iron stove that alternated between too hot and freezing'.[14] While they were there Helena, Christian and their party stayed at the British Embassy in Berlin.

While on her regular family visits to Germany, Helena did not forget her charitable interests. While staying with the Empress Frederick the previous year, both women had discussed in detail a cholera epidemic which had claimed many victims. It evidently gave her some food for thought, and shortly after her return to England she attended several meetings in connection not only with her nursing charities but also cholera committees.

Three years later she wrote an article, 'Trained Nurses and Nursing in England', which was published in *Woman and Home*. It gave her an opportunity to emphasise the vital importance of the care of the sick and suffering, and paid tribute to the pioneering work of Florence Nightingale. England would never forget, she wrote, that 'at a time when the strongest prejudice existed against women taking an active part in public life and work, she it was who, with the help of a few devoted followers, laid down the lines of a new career for women, which has proved to be of national importance and for the benefit of humanity in general.'[15] It was possible that Queen Victoria's fierce opposition to women nurses might have mellowed a little with age, but nevertheless one can only imagine what her reaction would have been to such an article. Helena may have quailed before the presence of the matriarch in her full fury, but she was never afraid to express her opinions in print – possibly secure in the knowledge that her mother, whose eyesight was failing, was never shown any newspapers or articles which she did not wish to see.

The last few years of the nineteenth century, and of Queen Victoria's life, were to prove a particularly trying time for her three younger daughters. She relied increasingly on Helena, Louise and Beatrice for support. Helena and Beatrice were as solid and dependable as ever, though they were still slightly intimidated by the all-pervading matriarchal presence. One of the Queen's ladies-in-waiting, Lady Lytton, noted in her diary while at Balmoral in the autumn of 1895 that 'Princess Christian always seems rather in awe of "dear Mama."'[16]

Louise was a difficult character, or in the words of Marie Mallet, another lady-in-waiting, 'so ill-natured I positively dread talking to her,'[17] and 'a dangerous woman, to gain her end she would stick at nothing'.[18] She had perhaps never fully recovered from a sleighing accident in Canada when her ear was badly injured; her husband was rumoured to be homosexual; and apparent infertility after having contracted tubercular meningitis during her adolescent years denied her the children which she would have loved to have. Jealous of her married sisters with their families, she also resented the fact that Queen Victoria trusted them more than she did her, she was given to making spiteful comments about their looks and intellect, and she also complained that they were conspiring in trying to keep her away from the Queen. She was also thought to be having affairs at various times with an assistant private secretary at court and two or three artists and sculptors. Long noted for a particularly sharp tongue, and given to spreading unfounded gossip about others, including her family, she was regarded with some suspicion by those closest to her.

Beatrice was frequently hurt by her behaviour, especially as she seemed to be flirting with Beatrice's good-looking husband Henry.

In November 1895 Reid, who had become a much-respected friend and confidante among the Queen's children, found himself required to intervene in an unfortunate personal situation which was steadily getting worse. Beatrice sent for him to speak about Louise's relations with Sir Arthur Bigge, who had just been appointed as the Queen's private secretary as successor to Sir Henry Ponsonby. Louise's relations with Bigge, her younger sister insisted, were 'a scandal and something must be done'. Helena, various other members of the family, and in particular Lady Bigge, were reported to be either very angry or else 'in despair about it'. According to Helena, Louise 'had ruined relations of others before and must not be allowed to do so again.'[19]

However, Helena was not considered blameless by everyone, and the sometimes sharp-tongued Marie Mallet regarded her as being 'not quite safe' because of 'her violent opinions and very often absurd tirades'.[20] A few reassuring conversations with Lady Bigge helped to solve the problem, but it was not the end of the matter as far as the princesses were concerned. Louise complained bitterly to Reid that the Queen, Helena and Beatrice were all being very unkind to her, and that they 'had laid their heads together' to ruin her position at Court.

While Helena was in a position to distance herself from the matter, there was evidently some lingering bitterness between her two younger sisters. Two years later, by which time Henry was dead and unable to defend himself, having gone to take part in an ill-fated African military campaign and succumbed to fever before he could return home, Louise said that he had 'attempted relations with her',[21] which she had very properly declined, and he was therefore trying to expose her and Bigge out of revenge, by spreading false rumours that they were having an affair. The general feeling was that the unhappily married Louise had possibly had a mild but basically innocent if ill-considered flirtation with Bigge; that Beatrice, who suspected that something must be going on between her husband and her sister, was angry enough to make a fuss about something relatively trivial; and that a spurned Henry had sought revenge by creating mischief. The latter may have been part of the reason why Henry, aware that he had at best made himself look foolish and at worst disgraced himself, had made amends by removing himself from a fraught domestic situation for a short time by volunteering to take part in an ostensibly glorious, but in fact foolhardy, expedition with the army overseas, and died without having had a chance to prove himself as a soldier.

Helena did not need to get involved in petty squabbles and jealousies between her younger siblings, for at the time she had other family worries. Her husband had recently lost an eye through an accident which could be ascribed in part to the folly of a family member who as an experienced military man should have known better; her elder son was on active service with the army abroad; her elder daughter who would have made such a model wife was single, and her younger daughter's marriage was not proving a success. Above all, her ageing, often peevish mother and sovereign increasingly needed and relied on her.

Although Helena was on the whole quite a tough personality and not easily bowed, the combination of circumstances could sometimes be too much for her. While the Queen and others were all too readily inclined to accuse her of hypochondria and her husband of making too much of a fuss of her, too little allowance was made for Helena's depression, and it was therefore hardly surprising that she relied perhaps more than was wise on opiates and other stimulants.

According to Reid, Helena was 'kindly if indiscreet', but he thought that she tended to suffer from numerous 'imaginary ailments'. By the last decade of the century her reliance on opium, laudanum and perhaps other dubious narcotics was becoming of increasing concern to those around her, especially her mother and her husband. In November 1894 both of them spoke to Dr Reid about the problem. On rare occasions, even during visits to the family, she would shut herself in her room all day and refuse to come out for anybody. Reid had been at Balmoral with Helena at around this time when he thought she 'was rather queer'. She would come and chat to him in his room, while both of them smoked. To do so openly while the disapproving Queen was around was not feasible, and even royal princesses were not expected to indulge in public. Reid thought that she was being prescribed excessive and unnecessary amounts of drugs by the other physicians she was consulting. He admitted to finding her 'a great bore', although in fairness to her this may have been at a time when she was having particularly pressing problems with her family and just needed a sympathetic person to talk to, as did her sisters and even her mother from time to time.

Although Christian had rarely spent more than a day or two with his wife in Germany while she was visiting the spas, in August 1895 he told her that he was going to accompany her on her journey to Nauheim. According to Emily Loch, she was rather irritated by his decision, perhaps as she had not expected him to join her and she felt that this sudden last-minute change in his plans would cause alterations to her routine. Like her mother and indeed the rest of the family, she did not always take kindly to disruption of her plans at short notice. Despite her insistence that he really did not need to come, he travelled with her and their suite, taking his dog Hans. Shortly after their arrival at the Villa Anna and Christian's temporary departure to another location nearby, their canine friend caused a problem when he became ill and a vet had to be consulted. Then he went missing, resulting in Helena and Emily Loch having to look and call for him, but in vain. Next day Hans turned up, exhausted and clearly not well. When Christian arrived back at the villa, he was very concerned about the little creature, who was subsequently cared for with great tenderness but to no avail. Within a few days the dog was dead.

During their stay at Nauheim Helena continued to consult doctors, take her baths and enjoy 'little drives' around the area. She and Emily also paid a visit to Kronberg, where Friedrichshof, her sister the Empress Frederick's new home, was almost completed. In addition to this she also went to Wolfsgarten, where she spent some time with the young Grand Duke and Duchess of Hesse, the less than happily-married cousins Ernest and Victoria Melita.

Early in 1896, Helena was with the Queen at Cimiez. At the time the family were recovering from the shock of Henry of Battenberg's unexpected death on 20 January, and she helped to shoulder the newly widowed Beatrice's burden by answering some of the letters of condolence they had received. To a Professor Story, she wrote (29 January) that it was God's will, and her sister was 'admirable beyond words. Her wonderful firm faith is sustaining and helping her in this her hour of sorest need. Her patience, gentleness, submission, her courage and unselfishness are beyond all praise. But oh! it rends one's heart to see her.'[22]

She was still regularly consulting Dr Reid, who noted that she was 'very ill with facial neuralgia or pretending?' When she was still suffering from the same symptoms three days later, Reid was convinced that she was malingering, so he decided 'to stop all her narcotics and stimulants'.[23] After that she seemed to make a good if not complete recovery. One can only conclude that this was in part what was later recognised as 'cold turkey' on the part of her doctor, and also partly perhaps a tribute to the character of a strong personality who was well aware that determination, self-discipline and also the hard work which kept her mind occupied would be her salvation. In this she showed herself very much her father's daughter, if not her mother's as well. Although Queen Victoria's doctors could hardly be so bold as to say so directly, they doubtless thought her continual complaints about ill-health amounted to hypochondria at times. Like many a person before and since, part of the remedy for Helena was to be self-willed enough to 'give up', make the break and stop relying on medication.

At around this time she also had a recurrence of her eye trouble, and feared again that she might be losing her sight. Dr Reid discussed the problem with Professor Hermann Pagenstecher, who took charge of Helena's case, examined her and concluded that there was absolutely nothing the matter with her eyesight. He said that the symptoms of which she complained were 'simply the result of her nerves being shattered by stimulants and narcotics'.[24] These symptoms stopped rather suddenly on a family holiday on the French Riviera when she refrained or was perhaps forcibly stopped from taking the latter, and she was prescribed a spirit lotion to rub in instead. This was apparently a panacea which had neither any good nor bad effects, but she was convinced that it was or would be beneficial. She was so taken with it that she later obtained some bottles for the Queen in her later years when her eyesight was beginning to fail.

Although she could be selfish at times, the Queen was particularly concerned that this once most reliable daughter was perhaps not malingering after all, to the extent that she and Christian found it necessary to discuss the problem with Reid. It was unfortunate that the latter, a close friend of the ever lively but often sharp-tongued Louise, was inclined to be less than sympathetic to Helena. With some reluctance he prescribed her various solutions, but at length he lost patience with her, complained of her hypochondria, and withdrew the drugs and prescriptions altogether. Though she had already been making efforts to wean herself off them, it says a certain amount for Helena's self-discipline and determination as well as her strong constitution that she was able to put her dependency behind her and make what was apparently a full recovery. She also probably recognised that she needed to be fit and well for the sake of the members of her family who needed her most, particularly her mother in her last remaining years.

Recognising that his depression-prone mother needed diversions and other activities to keep her mind occupied, Christian Victor, who had become an experienced and enthusiastic photographer, suggested to her that she ought to take up the hobby as well. At around Easter he found an expert in the art, Miss Taylor, who helped to show her how to take shots, develop the films and make the prints. Emily Loch was sent to Windsor to obtain the necessary supplies. A busy weekend followed, with Helena taking views of Cumberland Lodge and the surrounding area. She was evidently very taken with this new pursuit, and soon ran out of supplies, so next day she and Emily went to Harrods in London together 'to get photographic liquids'.[25]

The last great occasion of Queen Victoria's reign was the diamond jubilee in the summer of 1897. Helena and Christian joined with members of the family in presenting her with a diamond sautoir chain to mark the occasion, and in attending the first service at St George's Chapel, Windsor, on 20 June, as well as at the great banquet at Buckingham Palace on the following evening. On the morning of 22 June Helena, the Empress Frederick and Beatrice breakfasted with their mother in the Chinese luncheon room at Buckingham Palace. Afterwards Helena and the Princess of Wales took their places in the state landau, drawn by eight horses, seated opposite the Queen in the procession from the palace to St Paul's Cathedral to attend the main service of thanksgiving. While the celebrations were at their height in London and Windsor, Helena went to Birmingham on 7 July to represent the Queen at the opening of the city's new General Hospital.

In the summer of 1899 Helena paid one of her regular visits to the Empress Frederick at Friedrichshof. The latter had not been well since a fall from her horse the previous autumn, and an examination by her physician soon afterwards revealed that she was suffering from cancer, though she was anxious to keep the news from her family at first. Helena returned to England just in time to see her beloved eldest son Christian Victor before his departure to go and fight in the war in South Africa. The Empress had told her daughter Sophie that while they were together in Germany her sister was 'in very low spirits'.[26] As he was leaving on active service, he allowed her to come and wave him off at the station. Neither of them could know that they would never see each other again.

It was only to be expected that another conflict involving Britain would call on her services in some way or other. Shortly after the outbreak of hostilities, she persuaded the Central British Red Cross Committee to provide funds for the building and equipping of a hospital train. A contract was signed in October 1899 with the Birmingham Carriage and Wagon Company, and completed within two months. Helena took an active interest in the construction of the vehicle, named the Princess Christian Hospital Train, and visited Birmingham to inspect the work in progress. She, the Queen and other members of the royal family contributed personally to the provision of some of the stores, and she helped to defray part of the cost, as did the Borough of Windsor. The seven-carriage train was transported to Durban, where it was reassembled on arrival in February 1900, lavishly equipped with medical supplies, and used to transport over 7,500 wounded soldiers.[27]

Naturally she would be extremely sympathetic to the plight of others with sons in the army overseas. That same month she wrote to

Colonel Mends of the King's Royal Rifles, a regiment with which Christian Victor had previously served. Private Thomson, a twenty-year-old soldier who was serving in South Africa, was apparently missing and his parents were extremely anxious as to his whereabouts. She also contacted the American Ambassador, and her royal status obviously helped to expedite enquiries. A month later, Private Thomson was found alive and well in Pretoria.

This first year of the new century was proving to be an unhappy one for the royal family. In May Queen Victoria celebrated her eighty-first birthday. Within weeks her spirits as well as her physical health were beginning to fail, and perpetual anxiety about the Boer war and military reverses for the British army was telling on her. Moreover the failing health and death of her second son and Helena's favourite brother Alfred, who had become Duke of Saxe-Coburg Gotha in succession to his uncle Ernest seven years previously, was a severe blow, especially as few of them had realised how unwell he was.

As someone who had suffered from and successfully fought her addictions, Helena had probably had more sympathy than the rest of them with Alfred, whose last years had been overshadowed by alcohol abuse as well as an increasingly unhappy marriage, boredom in a tedious German duchy which was no compensation for the naval service from which he had retired with some regret, and the suicide of his only son and heir, another Alfred, early the previous year. The family had been aware that he was suffering from cancer, but only on 27 July did the Queen receive a report which she had been anxiously expecting, to confirm that the doctors had sent an account which was 'very alarming'. They were all horrified on 30 July to learn of the assassination the previous day of Humbert, King of Italy, and further concerned at another telegram arriving at the same time to say the Duke was 'weaker and drowsy'.

It fell to Helena to receive yet another the following morning to tell them that he had passed away the previous evening, and break the news to their mother as she had finished dressing, that it was 'bad news, very bad news; he has slept away!'[28] Privately she was furious with Beatrice, whom she believed had been aware all along of the hopeless state of their brother's declining health but had concealed it from them all, perhaps for fear of upsetting the Queen too much.

The family were already aware that the Empress Frederick was also seriously ill. In September 1898 she had been injured after a fall from her horse while out riding, and soon afterwards a medical examination confirmed that she also had cancer. At one stage in October 1900 the doctors feared that she was dying, and Helena was sent for to come to her bedside and see her for what might be the last time. When she arrived the crisis had passed, but she, her brothers and sisters, and indeed her mother, knew that she did not have long left.

An even greater, and unexpected, sorrow was about to befall them. Like his late uncle Henry of Battenberg, Christian Victor had gone to serve in Africa, but once again it was not enemy action that would carry him off. He had fought with distinction in several battles during the campaign, had been appointed aide-de-camp to Lord Roberts in Pretoria, and was looking forward to returning home on leave in November. After organising an army cricket match in which he scored a century he felt unwell, and thought it was as a result of exerting himself too much in the game. However it turned out to be enteric fever, his condition worsened rapidly, and the doctors realised there could be no hope for him. On 29 October he received Holy Communion and then passed away. His request that, in the event of his death, his body should remain where he died as had been the case with his fellow soldiers was duly honoured, and he was interred in the Pretoria cemetery three days later.

'Poor dear Lenchen, poor Christian, who is abroad, and loved this son so dearly!'[29] Queen Victoria wrote at Balmoral in her journal, after Helena Victoria received the telegram and broke the tragic news to her. 'Aunt Lenchen's grief makes my heart bleed,' the Empress Frederick wrote to her daughter Sophie. 'He was her idol, and gave her such joy, and proved such a good steady boy.'[30] 'It is too terribly sad to have gone through such hardships and dangers,' the Queen wrote to the Empress Frederick, 'and not far from his return home to get that awful illness and be lost when all thought him safe.' Helena, she observed with admiration, 'bears up wonderfully.'[31]

Marie Mallet was impressed with the stoic way in which the bereaved mother bore up; 'I cannot say how much I admire her Christian fortitude and resignation; she is so brave but truly heart-broken, but for the Queen's sake she is determined to keep up and it comforts her to have some definite object in life so she will continue her good works...'[32]

The death of Christian Victor was an unexpected and devastating shock. Unlike his uncle Alfred, he had been a very popular young man, well liked and admired by everybody with whom he came into contact, and undoubtedly with a glowing future in front of him. Only two of the four sons of Helena and Christian had survived to adulthood, and now the most promising one was gone as well.

On 1 November a memorial service for the prince was held at St George's Chapel. Christian, who had just been summoned home while on a visit to family in Germany, Albert and Helena Victoria all attended, but Helena remained quietly at home with Marie Louise keeping her company. Yet tension remained in the family. What caused it is anyone's guess, but Emily Loch recorded in her diary next day that 'there were fearful péripéties (ups and downs) in the morning but after some explosions it got much better and the day became peaceful and pleasant'.[33]

Next day, ironically, Helena received her son's last letter. It included his description in fond detail of the last cricket match in Pretoria in which he had participated, and in which he speculated that the combination of the game and a mosquito bite had brought on an attack of fever, but he thought it was nothing to be worried about. Later that month his possessions were returned from South Africa. Helena gave Emily Loch the prayer book and Testament that he had had with him throughout the campaign.

Her troubles were far from over. Marie Louise had become anorexic and was increasingly unhappy with her husband Aribert, a homosexual who treated her with nothing but contempt, and life at the stuffy little German court. While she was visiting Canada in the autumn of 1900 she received a summons to return forthwith to Anhalt. Once Queen Victoria realised what was happening, she immediately countermanded it with a telegram to the Governor-General of Canada, the Earl of Minto, saying, 'Tell my granddaughter to come home to me, V.R.'[34]

This separation resulted in the exchange of much angry correspondence between the German Emperor and Empress on one hand, and members of the British royal family on the other. At length the normally placid Christian was so angry with his nephew that he threatened to come and appear before the Bundesrat or German federal council, in order to explain the reason why his daughter had separated from her husband. This silenced the Emperor, who was terrified of the scandal being made public and would not permit this under any circumstances.[35] The marriage was annulled in November 1900, and the princess spent the rest of her life in England, returning to what her grandmother called 'a state of single blessedness'.

To add to these sorrows, it was increasingly evident that the Empress Frederick, now too ill to pay the final visit to England which she so desperately wished to make, was unlikely to live for more than another few months.

Helena and Christian were probably unaware, and fortuitously so, of another source of sadness and even scandal at this time which could hardly even be acknowledged in Victorian England. Their younger son Albert, who was serving with the Prussian army, had had an affair in Berlin with 'a lady of high birth'. As a result she gave birth to his daughter, born on 3 April 1900 in Liptovský Mikuláš, Hungary. The child, named Valerie Marie, was placed almost immediately with a German couple of Jewish origin, Anna and Rubin Schwalb.

About ten days before his death in 1931 Albert wrote her a letter in which he fully admitted his paternity. By this time she was married, to Ernst Wagner, a lawyer, but this ended in divorce and in 1939 she married Engelbert-Charles, Duke of Arenberg. As marriages between Aryans and Jews were prohibited, she obtained a statement from her aunts Helena Victoria and Marie Louise which acknowledged her paternal lineage. She died in Nice in August 1953, probably by her own hand.[36] A death certificate issued by the authorities in Nice does not record a cause of death.

Her mother, and thus Albert's lover, was rumoured to have been a Baroness Bertha von Wernitz, who died the day after giving birth, although no reliable evidence has been produced to confirm it. It was ironic that Helena and Christian thus only had one illegitimate grandchild, but how much contact, if any, they ever had with her is unknown. It has been suggested that Helena may have learnt about it later in life, but if so there is nothing to show how she reacted to such news. Otherwise, her daughters were almost certainly the only relatives who were ever let into the secret.[37]

Marie Louise attended her niece's burial at Enghien, Belgium, two months after her death The press faithfully reported her visit there, but gave no explanation about the reason for her presence.

The court and family spent Christmas 1900 at Osborne in a mood of almost unrelieved gloom. It was exacerbated by one more bereavement, the sudden death in the small hours of 25 December of Jane Churchill, who had been one of Queen Victoria's favourite ladies-in-waiting. From her island home the Queen dictated what was to be one of her last letters to Beatrice, to the Empress Frederick, telling her sadly that 'Poor Lenchen, Christian and their children have borne up wonderfully, but poor Christian is terribly aged.'[38]

- 6 -

'A great comfort to me'
1901-14

As 1901 dawned, Her Majesty's strength was plainly ebbing. Part of the duties of Helena and Beatrice as her assistants included answering the many telegrams, letters and cards of congratulation that arrived at Osborne for the beginning of the new year. But like the rest of the family, they must have been increasingly aware that this would be for the last time, as Mama would certainly not see another. On Sunday 13 January the Queen, who had kept her journal so faithfully for nearly seventy years, dictated the final entry, as she had been doing for the previous few days. She noted that after a fair night 'Lenchen came and read some papers,' and then they and Beatrice went out for a short drive. A short service was held in the drawing room, after which she rested, 'then did some signing, and dictated to Lenchen.'[1] Her third daughter's name is thus the last to be mentioned in her journal.

As the eldest of the siblings at home, around the middle of the month Helena took on the responsibility of sending daily reports on their mother's condition by telegraph to the Prince of Wales at Marlborough House. Reid thought that she was taking far too sanguine a view, and playing down her mother's illness, as if in denial as to how close to death the sovereign really was. On 17 January George, Duke of York, noted in his diary that his father told him that the Queen had had a slight stroke that morning; 'He got a cipher telegram tonight from Aunt Helena saying that her condition was precarious but no immediate danger.'[2]

Reid had for some time been maintaining close contact with the Queen's eldest grandson, the German Emperor William, and he secretly sent a telegram to Berlin advising the Emperor that her condition was giving cause for concern. He left his capital as soon as he could, sailed for England and arrived at Victoria Station on the afternoon of 20

January. Helena and Beatrice were both alarmed to learn that he was on their way to Osborne. As the Duke of Connaught had been in Berlin representing the family at celebrations for the bicentenary of the Hohenzollern dynasty, they assumed that their brother, not the doctor, had taken it on himself to tell the Emperor. The sisters had both suggested that it would not be right for their nephew to come, fearing that his arrival along with that of his suite would only cause havoc at such a time, and also that for him to come to his grandmother's bedside so suddenly would alarm her, but they were overruled.

As a doctor, Reid was more aware of the likelihood that for his illustrious and increasingly frail patient, any illness would be her last. Helena, his wife Susan believed, had 'shut her eyes wilfully to the truth for so long, that now it is a shock'. The Reids thought that her behaviour was bordering on hysteria, and that she seemed determined that the Prince of Wales should not come to Osborne just yet, the reason again being that his sudden appearance would alarm their mother and make her realise that she was surely dying. Louise, who had always been much closer to her eldest brother than to her sisters, was irritated by their attitude, and did not hesitate to tell others. To members of her husband's family, she would complain bitterly that their mother was 'deluded' by Helena and Beatrice into believing that she was in better health than she really was. Yet in all fairness to both of the latter, it would have hardly done for them to say anything else to Mama. However the Reids felt obliged to overrule them, and the Prince was accordingly summoned.[3]

Despite Helena's attitude, Mrs Reid thought she had more feeling than her sisters. Beatrice, she was surprised to see, gave the impression of being relatively unconcerned about her mother's condition. According to Reid himself, Louise was cooperative enough, eager to help in any way she could, but was as usual 'much down on her sisters', and he hoped she would not stay long, 'or she will do mischief!'[4] This was clearly the last thing any of them needed at such a solemn time.

By the morning of 22 January, which was ironically Christian's seventieth birthday, the Queen was plainly losing ground. Christian had been at Cumberland Lodge, unaware how ill his mother-in-law was until he received a telegram that morning from the Prince of Wales, summoning him to Osborne at once. For much of the day members of the family gathered round her bedside in a solemn vigil. Helena, Louise and Beatrice kept on telling her who was beside her, as she was too blind to make out anybody's faces and was only semi-conscious for part of the time.

Although he was standing there with the rest, they deliberately omitted the German Emperor's name. Reid whispered to the Prince of

Wales that he thought they should tell her that her grandson was there, at which the Prince beckoned to Reid so as to draw him out of earshot and explained that they all feared it would excite her too much if she knew he was present. Towards noon, Reid told the Emperor he would take him in alone. William was highly displeased that everyone's name in the room had been mentioned but his. Reid nodded, asked and was granted permission from the Prince of Wales to take the Emperor in on his own to see his grandmother.

Once or twice towards the middle of the afternoon the Queen rallied slightly, but by about 4 p.m. she was clearly sinking. At 6.30 p.m., she breathed her last.

It had long been clear that the death of Queen Victoria would be a major life-changing event for her surviving children in England. As the eldest of the three sisters who had faithfully acted as her personal assistants for so many years, Helena found the new chapter in her life a difficult one to adjust to. As she sat in the second carriage of her mother's funeral procession at Windsor on 2 February with Louise, Beatrice, and King Leopold II of the Belgians, where Emily Loch reported afterwards that she was 'so wonderful,'[5] and as she and Christian attended the King's first state opening of Parliament twelve days later, part of her mind was doubtless concentrated on how different life would be without her presence constantly in the background.

During the aftermath of their mother's death, Helena spent a good deal of time at Windsor Castle with Beatrice, often working until very late in the evening as they sorted through the Queen's clothes and various small possessions. Some keepsakes, comprising collections that had accumulated over a long life, were distributed among the family and close friends. Among the most precious items about which they had to make a decision were all of the costumes the Queen had kept throughout her reign, among them her wedding dress, and the one she wore at her first council. Their wish that these latter items should be sent, appropriately, to the Victoria and Albert Museum at Kensington was fulfilled.

In her will, Queen Victoria had left No 78 Pall Mall, an imposing house on the south side, to Helena and Christian. It had been built for and named after the Duke of Schomberg, a Huguenot general who served under King William III, although subsequently renamed de Vesci House. It was purchased from Viscount de Vesci by the Commissioners of Works in 1900 for £6,000, and six years later it reverted to the name of Schomberg House. When less pressing commitments permitted, Helena, Helena Victoria and Emily Loch paid the house regular visits from

February 1901 onwards, particularly to see how it was taking shape as a team of workmen came to make it habitable. There were choices to be made as to which furniture could be moved there from Cumberland Lodge, purchase of further fixtures from Maples, as well as carpets and tea sets to be obtained elsewhere.

By April 1902 it was ready for them to move in, a process which was completed on the 20th when they were able to entertain King Edward and the new heir George, Prince of Wales, to tea. They were thus conveniently nearby for the major events leading up to the coronation of the King and Queen, scheduled to take place at the end of June but postponed until August in order to allow the King time to recover after an emergency operation. Now that Helena had a home in London as well as at Windsor, she was able to devote additional time to charities in the city, particularly hospital and institutions in the East End. She was such a frequent visitor there that at length she came to be known as 'our Princess'.[6]

Helena and Christian had never been particularly close to the brother and sister-in-law who were now King Edward VII and Queen Alexandra. Although there had been a common bond between the women who shared an interest in charitable activities, and to some extent the men and their love of shooting, as personalities they were very different, and the arguments about the duchies of Schleswig and Holstein, although long past, had opened a wound which continued to fester and would never be fully healed. Queen Alexandra could never completely forgive or forget what she had always seen as a gross insult to her father and the family in Christian becoming a member of her husband's family. Louise had generally got on well with her brother and his wife, and she was invited to Sandringham from time to time, but neither Helena nor Beatrice were ever shown the same hospitality. Arthur had likewise always been closer to Louise, and apart from Vicky, the Empress Frederick, who lived in Germany and was known to be dying, Helena now only had Beatrice. The King bestowed the Royal Victorian Chain on Christian, in recognition of 'personal services' to the sovereign. This was however little more than a formal gesture, a gift automatically awarded to several of the sovereign's male relatives.

In spite of this, it seems that the loss of their mother and the impending loss of their sorely-tried eldest sister brought brother and sister a little closer, even if only briefly. The King went to visit the Empress Frederick at Friedrichshof in February, as soon as he conveniently could after his accession, while Helena went abroad in the spring for a much-needed holiday. After the miserable winter of bereavements – the loss of her favourite brother, her favourite son and her mother within the space of less than six months – and bitter cold a change of scene was in order, even though for the first three weeks she had to endure what she called 'Siberian weather'.

On 14 March she set off for Calais with Emily Loch and Helena Victoria, travelling over the European mainland to Milan and Florence, encountering deep snow as they passed round the lake of Lucerne. Yet despite visits to old friends and old haunts, it was hard for her to shake off her feelings of low mood. 'One's sad desolate heart is ever with one,' she wrote to Emily Baird, 'though the outward surroundings of the beautiful nature here is soothing. Sorrow like mine will be life long.'[7]

Travelling north, on 20 April they reached Kronberg station en route for a visit to the Empress. Although she was in agony from cancer of the spine much of the time and virtually bedridden, on some days when the weather was good enough she was well enough to come out for a drive with her younger sister. At other times she was too weak to be moved from her room, so they would sit and talk, as Helena read to her.

She returned to England in the first week of May. It was a particularly sad birthday that year, her fifty-fifth and the first without her mother; 'on anniversaries such as this, and as yesterday's [which would have been that of the Queen], one feels one's sorrows more keenly than ever. But I know all is well with my loved ones, and I do thank God for that.'[8]

On 31 July she left England again for Germany so she could return to Friedrichshof, helping to nurse the Empress Frederick, now bedridden and in agony from cancer of the spine much of the time. 'Dear Aunt Lenchen's visit is a great comfort to me,' the Empress wrote to her daughter Sophie, Crown Princess of Greece, early that summer, 'she reads to me and looks after me most kindly.'[9] Her heart breaking, Helena reported back to her brother on their sister's last hours, telling him that she was altered beyond recognition. Her breathing had been very laboured, and she was only able to talk with difficulty and utter a few words at a time, speaking 'much of Mama, repeating over and over again, "oh how I miss her, she understood my sufferings."'[10]

To Helena, the dying woman dictated precise instructions for her funeral. She intended that there was to be no post-mortem, no embalming, no photographs or portraits of her after death, and no lying-in-state. She left instructions that her body was to be covered by the Prussian royal standard, the coffin closed and placed in the town church in Kronberg, and then moved for interment in the mausoleum at Potsdam. Her sufferings endured until she passed away, aged sixty, on 5 August 1901. It was partly thanks to Helena that her sister's wishes were carried out when the time came, and also partly thanks to her that King Edward VII was able to come and join other British, German and European royalties, Helena and Christian among them, at the funeral at Potsdam on 13 August. As her brother, it would have been difficult to deny him his rightful place at the obsequies, although at one stage Emperor William had threatened to try and exclude him.

At this sad time in which she had lost two siblings, a parent and an eldest child within little more than a year, Helena doubtless found some relief in busying herself as much as ever, working on behalf of her various charities. She was heavily involved with the YMCA and the NSPCC, and she also started a district nursing service in Windsor and the Military Nursing Service, interviewing volunteer nurses for South Africa personally, and supporting the Princess Christian Hospital Train. One source of annoyance came shortly after the start of the new reign, when she was obliged to resign the presidency of the Army Nursing Service to Queen Alexandra. Nevertheless she retained her presidency of the Army Nursing Reserve.

The RBNA gradually went into decline after the Nurses Registration Act, which was passed in 1919 allowing formal nurse registration after failed attempts between 1904 and 1918. The result was the Royal College of Nursing and the RBNA lost membership and dominance. Helena supported the proposed amalgamation of the RBNA with the new RCN, but that was unsuccessful when the RBNA withdrew from the negotiations. She remained active in other nursing organisations, and was President of the Isle of Wight, Windsor and Great Railway branches of the order of St John. In this position, she personally signed and presented thousands of certificates of proficiency in nursing, and gave papers at meetings on subjects such as First Aid against tropical diseases.

Helena was at the forefront of the royal ladies who had all been helping to establish the modern working role of a member of the royal family, the others being Louise and Beatrice, and Helen, the widowed Duchess of Albany. For the last few years they had worked tirelessly, and they made up a team as more or less full time working royals. During her brother's nine-year-long reign she continued to represent the family at various ceremonial and charitable functions. To cite only a few examples, in March 1903 she opened the Suffolk, Victoria Nursing Institute; in January 1905 she appeared at St George's Hall, Liverpool, where she was present at a meeting of the Liverpool School of Tropical Medicine, to hear a lecture on 'The progress of tropical medicine'; in June 1906 she laid the foundation stone of a sanatorium for consumptives at Benenden, Kent; and in March 1907 she laid the foundation stone of the new Central Public Library, Hackney, one of several similar institutions which was being built with funds provided by the philanthropist Andrew Carnegie. Rarely a few months, even weeks, went by without reports of her in the newspapers opening a sale, bazaar or exhibition somewhere, in aid of various good causes, or presenting prizes at a school in the London and Windsor areas.

Another of Helena's major preoccupations was that of overseeing the completion of suitable memorials to her eldest son. She and Christian had known that his dearest wish would be for those that were not purely ornamental but of some practical value as well. In 1902 two houses in Clarence Villas, Windsor, were acquired and converted into what was to become the Princess Christian Nursing Home in his memory. She and Christian thought it only fitting that any memorial to him should be one of service to his suffering fellow-beings, and it was a proud day for the family when it opened its doors to admit its first twelve patients.[11] The opening ceremony was held on 27 February with 'crowds of Doctors, Clergy and nurses', a prayer reading, a lesson and finally a blessing from Archbishop Randall Davidson. Everyone was then given a guided tour of the home and then served with tea. The guests left at about 5.00 p.m. but Helena stayed on, then went to the workmen's dinner which she had arranged for them at the White Hart.[12]

An official biography of the late prince was published. Edited by T. Herbert Warren, *Prince Christian Victor: The Story of a Young Soldier*, was compiled from letters from him to Christian and Helena, to Queen Victoria (and after her death bequeathed to Helena Victoria), and to George, formerly Duke of York, now the Prince of Wales. The other source material included his cricket book, shooting book and diaries. To his mother, its appearance in print was part of the process of keeping his name before the public.

There was another major solemn family duty which needed to be undertaken several thousands of miles away. On 20 August 1904 she and Helena Victoria, accompanied by Vice-Admiral Sir John Fullerton and Surgeon-General Sir William Taylor, set out for South Africa on the Union Castle liner *Walmer Castle*. Sailing from Southampton, after a peaceful and uneventful voyage, they reached Cape Town on 6 September to be greeted by welcoming crowds as they landed, and these continued to give then a hearty reception wherever they went. Special trains had been provided by the Cape Government Railways, the Central South African Railways and the Natal Government Railways, each of them supplying lavishly decorated timetables of the journeys. Among the attractions which had been laid on for the party included visits to Cecil Rhodes' house, the de Beer diamond mines at Kimberly, and then Robinson Deep gold mine near Johannesburg. They also visited the Victoria Falls, and rode across the Zambesi in a workman's cake, or 'Blondin', where the younger and more intrepid travellers were suspended hundreds of feet above the river in the position where the bridge was about to be built. At her age Helena did not go into the Blondin, as she felt it was not a suitable activity for her. She was content to watch from a suitable distance, her large hat and umbrella protecting her from the spray of water.

Yet it was no mere sightseeing trip, as she had gone there for a purpose. Several of the places which they visited, particularly in the Transvaal, were battlefields from the war, where she was given a full explanation of what had happened there. Although it must have been considered a sensitive issue, if not verging on the tactless to some, to have a senior representative of the royal family and thus of the victorious empire in their midst, she made a point of meeting and speaking with Boers and Britons, and the local community gave her an enthusiastic welcome. Among those whom she met were Louis Botha, who had been a general during the Boer War, was now regarded as the leader of the nation, and would shortly become the first Prime Minister of the Union of South Africa. General Jan Smuts refused to meet her, as he and his wife were still bitter over the outcome of the war, and even more so as one of their children had died in a British concentration camp. Some years later Smuts met Marie Louise on a visit by the latter to the Cape, and he told her that he had always deeply regretted his refusal.[13]

Helena's underlying reason for the journey had touched the hearts of many people there, particularly mothers who had lost loved ones on the field of battle. Naturally the most important part of the journey was a visit to her son's grave in Pretoria on 26 September, and she was allowed to see it during the early morning so that she could do so alone while it was still quiet. Later that day she returned with others, so she could say a last farewell. She presented a signed portrait to the florist who had always attended the grave, and personally thanked his children who had undertaken to place flowers regularly, and asked them to continue doing so. Before boarding the train and continuing to Johannesburg, she also left orders for some structural alterations to the tomb to be made.

Ironically, not long before her visit, two attempts had been made to remove the Prince's body from the grave. During one of these, the covering slab was broken, and quickly repaired just in time. A reward of £200 was offered by the Transvaal government for the apprehension of the perpetrators, but they went undetected and the honorarium was never claimed. It was believed that somebody may have been seeking a ransom, or alternatively that a Boer faction was keen to make a gesture that would embarrass the British authorities.

Later that week at a special ceremony, Helena presented the King's Colours to the Imperial Light Horse, the South African Light Horse, the Johannesburg Mounted Rifles, and the Scottish Horse, four of the volunteer regiments which had performed conspicuous service during the war. She also opened a Princess Christian Home for the care of elderly ladies.

Having travelled several thousand miles, and spending a little over two months away from England, the party arrived back in Southampton on 29 October, the fourth anniversary of Christian Victor's death. Although Helena might have felt she deserved a rest on her first evening home in England, she spent the time instead with her elder daughter, appropriately paying another visit to the Nursing Home at Windsor in memory of her son.

Now in his early seventies, Christian was leading an increasingly quiet life, although despite his advancing years he represented King Edward at select foreign functions. Among them were the celebrations in Berlin for the silver wedding of the German Emperor and Empress in 1906. From around this time onwards, however, he was ever more vulnerable to minor complaints and severe fatigue. While he still enjoyed inspecting the hounds at the start of the hunting season, going out on the hunt itself, and going out shooting, such activities made him increasingly tired and he had to curtail them accordingly. For the most part the couple continued with their uneventful existence at Cumberland Lodge, interspersed with occasional visits abroad, but less often than formerly.

On 6 May 1910 King Edward VII died, aged sixty-eight, at Buckingham Palace. Having been confined to bed with heart trouble only at the very end when he was too ill to protest that he should be up and working, he lay barely conscious with only his wife and doctors in his room. Helena and Christian were among the senior members of the family who waited for the sadly inevitable in an adjoining room, together with the Prince and Princess of Wales, shortly to become King George V and Queen Mary, the King and Queen's two elder daughters Louise, Princess Royal and Duchess of Fife, and the unmarried Victoria, and also Helena's sister Beatrice. What Helena's thoughts were on the imminent passing of the brother she had always looked up to but to whom she had never really been that close can only be imagined. His death, however, conferred a status of seniority on her in the royal family in that she was now the eldest of the four surviving children of Queen Victoria and Prince Albert.

Although she was now in her mid-sixties, there was no perceptible slowing down in the charitable activities which she regularly undertook. During 1911 she chaired meetings of the Ladies' Association of the Hospital for Women, Soho Square, the South African Colonisation Society, and the Soldiers' and Sailors' Help Society. In addition to these she opened the King Edward Memorial Hospital, Ealing, in July, and three months later she went to Portsmouth dockyard she launched a new dreadnought battleship, *George V*. Emily Loch, who accompanied her royal mistress, was very impressed as she watched her christen the ship, 'after which the blocks were knocked away by hundreds of men – then they were called out; the Princess severed the cords with chizel [sic] and hammer – the weights dropt and almost the same second the huge ship moved and slid down into the sea.'[14]

It was a busy year with two major ceremonial events as well. One was the unveiling to a statue to Queen Victoria in front of Buckingham Palace that spring, attended by the royal family including the German Emperor. The second was the coronation in June of King George V and Queen Mary, at which Helena rode in a carriage with her sisters Louise and Beatrice, and the Princess Royal, the new King's eldest sister Louise, Duchess of Fife.

That autumn a decision was taken that Cumberland Lodge should be wired for electric light, which would replace the old gas system. When the work was begun, it was found that the building was suffering from dry rot. An inspection by the Sanitary Adviser to the Office of Works advised that in its present state it constituted a serious risk to health, and that it also presented a fire risk because of the large amount of timber that had been used in the construction of the house. The solution lay in a partial rebuilding, at an estimated cost of about £10,000, and the family had to move out for a year, returning to Frogmore House. At their time of life they found the upheaval rather an inconvenience, and Helena was insistent that they should be able to return before the end of the following year. She wrote to the Surveyor-General (3 September 1911), that she and the Prince wished 'the matter should be taken in hand at once – for I do not think we could arrange to be longer away than till October 1912.'[15]

The major alterations to the house undertaken included the moving of the main staircase, raising and renewing of the roof, the provision of additional bedrooms for servants, and the replacement of the wooden floors with concrete ones covered with parquet in the main rooms and passages. While new basements were being constructed, long-forgotten underground passages were found leading to Great Meadow Pond near Windsor Castle.

A small hand-powered passenger lift was installed for the benefit of Christian, who was now in his early eighties and finding it increasingly difficult to manage stairs. It was not a success, and he thought it almost useless as it was so slow. Additional lighting was provided outside the house, particularly as a security precaution in the event of 'suffragette raids'.[16] The family would have been an undeserving target of any militant protests. Leaders of the movement were probably unaware that, unlike her late mother, Princess Christian of Schleswig-Holstein was sympathetic to the issue of votes for women, although it would have hardly been appropriate for the King's aunt to make her views publicly known on such a controversial issue of the day. While in her younger days she might have been renowned as a true conservative (if not a Conservative), particularly in her detestation of the Liberal Prime Minister Gladstone which she shared with Queen Victoria, with regards to her views on opportunities for women she was at heart probably more radical than several of her nephew's ministers.

While the rebuilding was in progress, Helena was distressed to hear rumours from officials in charge of the alterations that they were under the impression Cumberland Lodge was being rebuilt for some other unnamed royalty, thought to be Queen Mary's brother. The rather tactless implication was that Prince Christian, now in his early eighties, did not have much longer to live.

Although she had been given to understand that Queen Victoria had allowed her to stay in the house for the rest of her life, Helena had nothing in writing to confirm the arrangement. In order to put her mind at rest she consulted her nephew, King George V. A letter from his private secretary, Lord Stamfordham, made it clear that when the alterations were completed, Prince and Princess Christian would continue to live there, 'and no one but HM himself has anything to do with the future occupancy of the house'.[17] She had already given some thought to the situation that would arise on the death of her husband, thinking that it would probably be more economical for her to leave Cumberland Lodge and settle in a smaller country residence instead. Keen to set her mother's mind at rest, Helena Victoria had contacted the King, who assured her that her mother would be able to live there until her death if she so wished.

- 7 -

'My loneliness and desolation' 1914-7

The Liberal government which had swept overwhelmingly to power in 1906 did so with a mandate for radical change. Several new welfare initiatives and legislation came into existence, and in these Helena took a keen interest.

In March 1913 she attended the annual meeting of the Association for Promoting the Training and Supply of Midwives, held at the Wesleyan Central Hall, Westminster. Another of those present, Dr Christopher Addison, a Liberal Member of Parliament, gave an account of the working of the Insurance Act as it affected maternity benefit. When he had finished, she asked why it was that benefit payments should be refused to a woman who had been in a private maternity home. A case had recently come to her notice of someone who had had great difficulties in obtaining the money due to her. Dr Addison replied that women in such cases were indeed entitled to the benefit, but it would not be paid until she had left the home. When another lady present pointed out that she was aware of instances of the husband getting the money and spending it without his wife ever seeing a penny, Helena asked how they could guard against that happening again in future. Addison admitted that the rule should be altered, and she endorsed his decision, agreeing that the procedure was 'very confusing and difficult', and that 'there are wheels within wheels'.[1]

Early in 1914 she found herself with regret in the position of having to resign as President of St George's Hospital. An independent enquiry was being made in order to investigate charges which had been brought against the administration of the hospital by treasurers. Two of them, the Earl of dean of westminPlymouth and Mr A. William West, had previously submitted their resignations, but these were temporarily withheld until after Helena had done likewise.

On 21 January she wrote to the Board of Administration, advising them that she was anxious that the inquiry should take place 'in order that I might become cognizant of all sides of the late differences of opinion which up to the present time I have been ignorant of. Certain governors, however, whilst not objecting to answering any questions put to them, distinctly state they do not recognize any authority on my part, nor will they consent to abide by any decision arrived at as a result of such an inquiry.' Such a procedure, she said, 'would be useless, and it therefore falls to the ground.' It was with the deepest regret that she found herself obliged to resign her position, as she had taken such an interest' in the activities of the hospital for so long.[2]

On 2 May 1914 her brother-in-law Lord Lorne, Duke of Argyll, died peacefully after a short illness. Time had had a healing effect on the differences between Louise and her husband, who had lived at Kent House, near Osborne, but not apparently between the two sisters. Helena had offered to go and be with her during the first few painful days of widowhood, and she was disappointed if not completely surprised to be informed that her presence was not wanted. As she explained to Lorne's brother-in-law Ralph Glyn, who had been similarly excluded; 'there are natures – who when trials and griefs come to them – somehow shrink from the very ones who are most dear to them!' Louise evidently thought that her elder sister was longing to come into her house just to interfere and alter everything. Regretfully Helena complied with her wishes, saying to Ralph's wife Mary that she would 'go any moment if she w[oul]d have me but you know the difficulties and I don't want to put myself forward in any way.'

Younger members of the royal family looked with distaste on such behaviour between the sisters at such a solemn time, and what they thought was developing into an undignified spat or could very easily do so. Their niece Princess Louis of Battenberg commented disdainfully that 'I don't want to grow like "the Aunts"'.[3] It was, however, no more than a temporary difference between two very determined royal ladies of the senior generation, which was soon smoothed over.

Although Helena's health had seemed better for the last few years, there were still occasional minor dispositions, and these could occur at the most inconvenient of times. 4 June 1914 had been declared 'Helena Day', with roses being sold to the public at Slough and Windsor, and all proceeds going to local charities. People had decorated the outside of their houses and residential streets with flowers, while public buildings in the towns were also suitably adorned for the occasion. Much to her disappointment, she was prevented from making a personal appearance by a 'severe sick headache' in the morning, and had to send her apologies to the Mayor. Nevertheless 70,000 roses were sold, and a total of £452 was collected, of which £363 was passed to Helena for her various good causes.[4]

Within the next few years, as the long-feared European tensions exploded into armed conflict, there would indeed be many a call for further efforts on behalf of 'good causes'. By midsummer, the threatening political situation between England and Europe, which had been increasingly uncertain for the last few years, was looking ever more precarious.

The catalyst came on 28 June when the heir to the throne of Austria-Hungary, Archduke Francis Ferdinand and his wife Sophie, were assassinated while on a visit to Sarajevo, the capital of Bosnia. On 27 July Helena warned Emily Loch that they would be unable to make their usual expedition to the continent as previously planned 'because of the war scare'.[5] Scare turned to grim reality a few days later, when on 4 August Britain declared war on Germany, and on 12 August on Austria.

Like most of the family, Helena and Christian were deeply affected by the division of family loyalties. Helena had probably enjoyed better relations with the German Emperor and Empress than any of her siblings, with the possible exception of the Duke of Connaught, but now they were officially enemies. Their only surviving son Albert, who had never really wanted to be a German prince, had been adopted as heir to his childless uncle Ernest Gunther, Duke of Schleswig-Holstein. Helena and Christian had agreed to this, to his living in Germany and to his taking German nationality, but with some reluctance. Now that he was resident there, and responsible for supervising the family estates in Silesia, he was in English eyes an enemy alien. He had served at one time as a member of Emperor William's bodyguard, and although he had officially retired from the army four years previously he was obliged to place his services at the disposal of his sovereign. This he did with a heavy heart, and only on condition that for obvious reasons he would not be ordered to go and serve on the Western Front where he would be engaged in hostilities against the British.

Nevertheless it was a source of distress to his parents. 'Our only boy is with the German Army on the wrong side!!' lamented Helena, writing to Lady Augusta Montagu (20 August 1914). 'Oh! The sickening anxiety for so many dear ones out on the front – on <u>both</u> sides.'[6]

Fortunately Albert's desire to refrain from taking up arms against his own countrymen was respected when he was placed in charge of a camp for English prisoners. A year later the Prime Minister, Herbert

Asquith, was obliged to request that the King should order the removal of banners of enemy princes on display in Westminster Abbey. The King expressed his reluctance to do so, on the grounds that they were part of history, and he stressed that in particular his cousin Albert was not fighting on behalf of the Germans. This did not satisfy the popular clamour, and the banners were accordingly taken down and put into storage.

Although she had previously liked and respected her imperial nephew in Berlin, now that they were at war Helena was just as critical of him as the rest of the family in England. She held him partly responsible for the calamitous course of events, and she thought the Emperor 'must be quite mad to have lit such a conflagration'.[7] The German-born Christian's patriotism to his adopted country was never in doubt, and the now elderly man who had longed to go and fight on behalf of the fatherland against the French early in his married life was now as firmly British in his sympathies as anyone. During the war he followed daily reports on the progress of the war in *The Times* with interest, angrily muttering 'Zese blody Germans' to himself as he was reading. Whenever he saw a soldier around the Lodge, he called him indoors for a few friendly words, then made him a gift of cigars and cigarettes, and handed him half a crown. American nurses who were working in Windsor were regularly invited to come and join them for tea at the house.[8]

In time of war Helena's good works and efforts on behalf of charities were now more invaluable than ever, and she spent much of her time in meetings concerned with nursing, hospitals and medical supplies where they were needed. In 1915 the British Red Cross Society contributed £10,000 towards the building of the Princess Christian Red Cross Hospital at Englefield Green, overlooking Windsor Forest, and she collected the rest of the money. This new establishment comprised six pavilions, each containing twenty beds, and it was constructed in twelve weeks. It was handed over to the War Office in September 1915, and she was invited to perform the opening ceremony, with a group of overseas soldiers expected to arrive a few days later.

One way in which she was able to pull rank to good effect occurred when the wife of a gamekeeper at Windsor Great Park visited her. She was clearly very upset as her daughter had 'got into trouble' with her fiancé, who had been sent to France with his unit before the marriage could take place. The baby was due to arrive shortly, and there was no time to be lost. 'Leave it to me and I will deal with it,' Helena assured her without hesitation. As her daughters remarked, when they saw their mother put on her bonnet and shawl, they knew that she meant business. At once she went in person to the War Office in London, where she asked to speak to Sir John Cowans, the Quartermaster-General and a close personal friend of the family. Explaining the situation, she asked that he be given forty-eight hours' compassionate leave in order to marry the lady. Cowans tried to explain to her that it was impossible to withdraw him from his unit and bring him home, as he was holding a very important sector in the trenches opposite the enemy. But as with her various charitable meetings, Helena stood her ground and insisted. The soldier was granted his brief period of leave, and the wedding duly took place.[9]

Helena and Christian celebrated their own golden wedding anniversary in July 1916. It was ironic that in view of the age difference between them, theirs should be the only marriage among the children of Queen Victoria in which husband and wife both lived long enough to attain this milestone. Moreover, it was the first golden wedding to occur in the royal family since 1811, which had been that of King George III and Queen Charlotte – but the King's declining state of health at that time had not made any celebration possible. In the morning it began with a thanksgiving service in the chapel in Windsor Park, followed by endless congratulations, deputations from employees in the Park, and from Windsor, and a party to which they were all invited.

In the afternoon King George and Queen Mary came to tea. While they were all talking, a steward handed Helena a telegram from Margaret, Crown Princess of Sweden, who as a senior royal representative in a non-belligerent territory was perfectly placed to transmit royal messages between countries which were on opposite sides during the war. It read, 'William asks me to transmit to you his loyal and devoted good wishes to dear Uncle Christian and Aunt Helena on the occasion of her golden wedding.' They were astonished and touched that Emperor William, Britain's greatest foe at the time, should have remembered the anniversary of his favourite aunt in Britain, and passed on his good wishes through a cousin in a neutral country.

After they had all recovered from their astonishment, the King turned to Marie Louise and said that, thinking it over, her former husband Aribert had surely done her a service when he turned her out of house and home. What would she have done if she had still been living in Berlin during the war? She immediately answered that she would have run away to England, to which he replied with a twinkle in his eye that he would have had to intern her.[10]

That same year, a rival group to the Royal British Nurses' Association, the College of Nursing, was founded with the support of the medical royal colleges. It intended to act as a professional institution for trained nurses, pioneering the highest standards of education, practice and general working conditions. It initially received the support of the Royal British Nurses' Association, but its existence caused Helena some annoyance. In July 1917 she wrote to Miss Isabel Macdonald, Secretary of the Royal British Nurses' Association, about her treatment by the college, and the difficult situation in which she had been placed. As she was virtually the nominal President of the new College, she complained that she was told nothing by the College of its activities, and she was never contacted or asked about anything'. It placed her in a position of some difficulty 'about being in any way responsible for the College's actions, promises etc!' and wished the College Council could be made to understand.[11]

Next day she had further cause for annoyance. A statement was published in *The Hospital*, suggesting that the college was going to be given a royal charter. She demanded that this statement should be refuted, but without her being personally involved as she did not intend to attract any undue criticism of interference. It was her particular wish that the college should understand it was to be merged with the Royal British Nurses' Association, and not the other way round. She was also keen that the Trained Nurses' Auxiliary Find should be affiliated with the Helena Benevolent Fund and the Settlement Fund.

Mrs Bedford Fenwick fervently hoped that she would be nominated to represent at least one of the societies of which she was a member, on its affiliation with the Royal British Nurses' Association. Helena was always glad to welcome closer co-operation, writing to Mrs Fenwick (15 March 1918) that her 'one great object and desire has ever been to further the success and prosperity of our Associations, and to strengthen its [sic] position and to widen its sphere of influence'. For the societies and associations to be 'strong and united' was the only way to increase 'the welfare and prosperity of Trained Nurses as a great profession'. She would be pleased to accept Mrs Fenwick's nomination as she felt she could rely on her help and co-operation in everything relating to the good and welfare of the cause which they both had so much at heart. She was also sure that if all the affiliated Societies would support and aid their Associations and herself, 'and be united as one big strong body, we need have little fear as to the ultimate result'.[12]

An unforeseen difficulty arose the following month, when it appeared that Mrs Fenwick believed that she was going to become the Association's Vice-President. Helena had to write to Miss Macdonald (18 April 1918) that she had no objection to her being a member of the Council, but for her to assume the vice-presidency 'would have laid me open to attacks of all kinds and from all sorts of quarters'.[13]

A few days later Helena heard with delight that the National Union of Trained Nurses had agreed to affiliate with the Association. She was even more glad to hear that Mrs Fenwick had no influence with the nurses' union. Having found her a rather difficult colleague, the Princess wrote (20 April 1918) that she would certainly oppose any effort to get her on to the Executive Committee, as she would never agree to it. Everything she had done to make peace with her was done in order to help the nurses and the cause, but she was determined that Mrs Fenwick would not have any say in the internal management of the Association.[14]

In the summer of 1917, as the detestation of everything German intensified throughout the country and the press, King George was obliged to change the family name from Saxe-Coburg and Gotha to Windsor. In doing so he also had to do away with the family's various German titles and styles. Helena, Christian and their daughters now became Prince and Princess Christian, Princess Helena Victoria, and Princess Marie Louise, with no territorial designation.

By this time Christian, who had celebrated his eighty-sixth birthday in January 1917, was becoming increasingly frail. Cared for faithfully by his wife, daughters, and nurses from the Princess Christian Hospital in Windsor, he was confined to his room at Cumberland Lodge or in London for much of the time. In the autumn he was ill with a severe attack of bronchitis, and the family knew that the end could not be far off.

On 27 October, the anniversary of the death of their eldest son, the King and Queen came to visit Helena and Christian at Schomberg House. As he knew that he was dying, he was clearly delighted to see them for what he sensed would be the last time. At around 6 p.m. next day, with his wife and daughters at his bedside, he passed away peacefully.

Once again it was to her lifelong friend Emily Baird to whom Helena as a widow poured her heart out, as she thanked her for her letter of sympathy.

> You know how happy we were, and can understand what my loneliness and desolation are without the loving companion of over 51 years. But, I thank God for the eternal peace and blessedness which is his now, and in God's own good time I shall go to him.[15]

Christian's funeral was held at St George's Chapel, Windsor, on 1 November, with Helena Victoria, Marie Louise and King George as chief mourners. Helena did not attend, but spent the day quietly at Schomberg House. She had requested that no flowers should be sent, in order that unnecessary expense at a time of war might be avoided.

On 4 November a memorial service for Christian took place at the Royal Chapel near Cumberland Lodge, with Marie Louise present, as well as various residents and employees on the Crown estate. In his address, the Reverend H.O. Moore told the congregation that the Prince had lived a quiet life for many years, 'not without heavy sorrows, but on the whole a life serene and peaceful, enriched by a strong sense of duty and by family affection'.[16]

Twelve months later, another letter from Emily Baird at the end of her first year of widowhood elicited a response from Helena on very similar lines:

> It is so dear of you to have thought of me on yesterday's anniversary. I always feel that every day is anniversary, bringing with it dear and precious memories. One thanks God daily for the everlasting rest and blessedness of our loved ones.[17]

- 8 -

'Devoted to humanitarian and to womanly duties' 1917-23

The first few months of Helena' life as a widow were made no less easy by ongoing problems with the Commissioners. They seemed prepared to suggest that she and her unmarried daughters ought to be asked to leave Schomberg House and Cumberland Lodge, because of the expense of running her households. At the very least, it was inferred that the latter property had come with the largely honorary post of Ranger of Windsor Park as held by the late Prince Christian. Now that he was deceased, it was only fitting that the Princess should contribute to the expenses.

Helena and her Comptroller, Captain Liddell, accordingly produced a signed letter from Queen Victoria, dated 14 July 1888, in which she had stated that she granted the use of the Lodge to her daughter for life. This naturally settled the matter and Sir Frederick Ponsonby, King George's private secretary, confirmed that His Majesty had agreed there would be no 'variation of the conditions on which the house has hitherto been held'.[1] At her time of life she had no desire to contemplate yet another upheaval, and she was relieved at being able to live out her years in the place which she regarded as home.

Supported faithfully by her daughters, Helena survived her husband for another five and a half years. The four years of war came to an end with the armistice in November 1918, but not before there was one great and quite unforeseen grief to the family. On 21 July 1918 Helena and her daughters were at Windsor Castle, preparing to have lunch with King George and Queen Mary. Normally the most punctual of people, this time they were half an hour late. When they arrived, the King looked so stricken with grief that Helena assumed that there had been some catastrophic defeat on one of the battlefields. When she asked gently whether the news was very bad, he replied that it indeed was – but it was not what she thought. He had just been told that his cousin 'Nicky', the former Tsar of Russia, his wife Alix, their five children and servants, held as captives by the Bolsheviks at Ekaterinburg, had all been murdered.[2] Under such circumstances the lunch could hardly have gone ahead, and it was accordingly cancelled.

Five months later, the German army surrendered, and 'the war to end wars' was over. On 26 November, Helena and her surviving siblings were among those in attendance at a thanksgiving service for victory at St John's Church, Clerkenwell, led by the Archbishop of York.

By now several charities that had some connection with countries in Africa, and with the needy who were suffering as a result of the war in Europe, were among Helena's main interests, and in many of these she was ably assisted by Emily Loch. In October 1922, both of them were present at meetings set up for two South African charities, a fund for starving refugees in Greece, and a Red Cross meeting for the Russian Relief Fund.[3]

By this time Helena had bowed to the pressure of advancing years, and was content to take less of a lead and hand on the torch to others. One of the last times she addressed an audience was when she chaired a meeting at Portland Place in November 1921 in her capacity as President of the Homes of St Giles for British Lepers. Addressing all those present, she appealed to everyone in the country to come to the aid of a number of afflicted people who suffered from this disease, the disabilities of which forced them to shun the company of others. Most of them, she pointed out, had contracted the disease in the service of their country abroad.[4]

Another charity with which she became involved was the setting up of the Helena Club in Lancaster Gate. In October 1922 she informed Marie Louise that she had received £7,000 to buy and equip a house in the Paddington area of London. It aimed to provide facilities for women who were engaged in earning their livelihood, and for women who had formerly been in the armed services. According to the incorporation document, it was for the benefit of women who at any time 'enrolled for full-time service in any corps under the direction of a British Government department'.[5]

As was only to be expected, she remained active with her good works and committees almost to the end of her days. In her capacity as President of the Princess Christian College in Manchester, which had been established in 1901 and was now one of the senior institutions for the training of ladies as children's nurses, she was a joint signatory alongside the Chairman, Secretary and Treasurer, to a letter published in *The Times* on 8 February 1923. This drew attention to the importance of a career in nursing for girls and young women with university education, who despite their qualifications were still finding it ever more difficult to seek work in an overcrowded employment market. Nursing, the letter said, was one of the very few careers for women in which demand exceeded supply, and in which the applicant had considerable freedom of choice. The training and experience fitted girls not just for home life but also for positions of public responsibility, such as becoming matrons in schools, day nurseries, or taking up other branches of welfare work. It would also provide opportunities for travelling, as demand for lady nurses was not confined to the British Isles.[6] As with the *Woman and Home* article nearly thirty years earlier, in putting her name to what was a comparatively bold and forward-looking document, Helena was certainly not her mother's daughter.

By this time she was ageing badly and her health was increasingly poor. At the beginning of the new year she suffered from heart trouble, followed by influenza, and the Court Circular the following month stated that she had recovered 'and has resumed her normal life and occupation'.[7] While she was no longer in a position to be quite as active on her committees as she was in younger days, she remained in spirit at least as tireless a patron of charitable organisations as ever. In February she gave her patronage to a concert to be held at Carlton House Terrace the following month in aid of St Barnabas Hostels, France, established and maintained by voluntary contributions for those of slender means who wished to visit the graves of relatives fallen in the war. With Queen Olga of the Hellenes and Grand Duchess Xenia of Russia, she also gave similar support to a dance in aid of the Russian Refugees Association at Chesham House that month.

On 26 April the King's second son Albert, Duke of York, married Lady Elizabeth Bowes-Lyon at Westminster Abbey. Helena and her daughters were among guests at the party held at Buckingham Palace three days previously, as well as at the wedding and the reception afterwards. It was the last of many great royal occasions during her life which she would attend.

Two days later, she was complaining about her head. At the beginning of May she had another minor heart attack, and a nurse came to stay and be on hand when necessary. A heavy cold turned into influenza, but on 18 May she was well enough to leave the house, and she was driven to Kensington Palace so she could go and stay with Beatrice for ten days. Helena Victoria, who had been staying at Schomberg House, came to see her every day.

After she returned home her daughters came to nurse her, while the ladies-in-waiting took on the task of writing her letters. Two short thank-you notes to Emily Baird from that same month survive, one from Lady Edmonstone acknowledging with affection the receipt of a bouquet of lilies, and one from Emily Loch for good wishes on her birthday. The second mentioned that the princess had been very unwell following a second attack of illness, and was 'rather better, but very much pulled down',[8] so she would not be allowed to leave her room or see the many friends and relations who had arrived. Among those who were allowed to come and pay their respects were the widowed Queen Alexandra, with whom past differences had long since been forgotten and forgiven, and her younger sister, Marie Feodorovna, Dowager Empress of Russia, who was staying in England at the time.

Although she was now seriously unwell, Helena still did not neglect or forget her obligations to the many charities which had relied on her efforts for so long. It was with regret that she sent her apologies to the Society for the Overseas Settlement of British Women, explaining that she was unable to attend the meeting of the women's branch committee at Central Hall, Westminster, on 28 May, or the National Society of Day Nurseries for a conference to be held at Carnegie Hall on the next day.

On 31 May a bulletin signed by Lord Dawson of Penn and three other doctors announced that she had had a heart attack the previous day, following influenza. Further bulletins appeared in *The Times* during the next ten days, each one reporting that her condition caused anxiety, or that a slight improvement had not been maintained, and that her strength was declining. What they did not reveal was that in fact she had fallen into a coma at the beginning of the month, and those closest to her were certain that she would not recover. On 4 June King George and Queen Mary cancelled their plans to appear at Epsom Races, and it was announced that His Majesty's dinner to the Jockey Club would not now be taking place. Out of respect in view of her illness the Royal Navy Club annual dinner was likewise cancelled.[9]

By the morning of 8 June it was evident that she was steadily losing ground. At 9.10 a.m. the next day, she passed away peacefully. That evening her coffin was carried from Schomberg House by ten guardsmen to the chapel at Marlborough House, and a vigil was kept all night by the Kilburn Sisters.

Many tributes were paid to her in public. In the House Commons on 12 June the Home Secretary, William Bridgeman, offered the condolences of Parliament to His Majesty, as he paid tribute to her efforts in the field of nursing, hospital work and other charities:

> Few people, perhaps, realise the amount of pioneer work which she did for the cause of nursing. Florence Nightingale planted, Princess Christian watered, and God has given an increase in a very wonderful way; for I think it is no exaggeration to say that the alleviation of the pain of thousands of sufferers in the war and in other ways has been very largely contributed to by the pioneer work which Princess Christian did in the quiet time which preceded the war.

In replying to his address J.R. Clynes, Labour Member of Parliament for Manchester Platting, spoke on behalf of the temporarily absent Leader of the Opposition:

> The sympathies of Princess Christian for the suffering were expressed in her sacrifices and in her services and sustained endeavours to alleviate those sufferings. She was devoted to humanitarian and to womanly duties and never wearied in well-doing, and for one so elevated in station and social position she has left a memory of acts of benevolence and kindly social service. She was devoted to humanitarian and to womanly duties and never wearied in well-doing, and for one so elevated in station and social position she has left a memory of acts of benevolence and kindly social service.[10]

Helena's funeral took place at St George's Chapel, Windsor, on 15 June. At the ceremony the King and her only surviving brother the Duke of Connaught walked immediately behind the coffin, with Helena Victoria, Marie Louise, and their aunts Louise and Beatrice following them as chief mourners, while soldiers from the regiment of Prince Christian Victor paid their respects by lining the steps of the building. In his address, the Dean of Westminster told the congregation that it had been 'her constant ambition to use aright the position which she had inherited for her country's good. Her strong personal traits were her peace of mind and inspiration for ceaseless benevolence and her thought for others.'[11] On the same day, memorial services were also held at Windsor Parish Church nearby, and in the chapel at Mount Vernon Hospital, Northwood, of which she had been a patron.

Helena's body was interred in the Royal Vault. She was laid to rest beside that of her husband at the Royal Burial Ground, Frogmore, after its consecration on 23 October 1928.

Within a few hours of his aunt's death, the King had taken care to assure the bereaved daughters that Schomberg House would now be theirs to live in for the rest of their days, as it had been in the case of their mother. They had many letters of sympathy to answer, a task with which Emily Loch was glad to assist. Two days after the funeral Emily Loch wrote to Emily Baird:

> Princess Helena is so brave for she has been her Mother's close companion for so many years, and it is a terrible sorrow and loss to her, though she does not fully know the extent of that loss yet, as you say the world is indeed poorer for her loss.[12]

Naturally, her charitable efforts were remembered with affection particularly in the town where she had lived for so long. In a graceful tribute the following year, the Dean of Windsor noted that 'Practically every single movement she started for the benefit of Windsor had become universal, and accepted as the normal thing in the charitable and philanthropic life of England.'[13] Through her efforts and committee work, she had made a lasting contribution to the welfare and training of nurses in Britain, and she had been patron or president of 123 organisations.[14]

The whole country was indebted to her, and to what *The Times* called 'A life of service', the words which headed her obituary in the newspaper. It noted that in times of war her help was never wanting, and that 'in the supreme trial through which we lately passed no one gave more steady or efficient help to the Red Cross and similar agencies than did Princess Christian'.[15]

The woman who had been born and raised a true Victorian princess, and who in her younger days had shared many of the typical prejudices of the age, had matured into a forceful, hard-working personality determined to do good. In this she was anything but a typical Victorian. A tireless hands-on patron of numerous charities, she also spoke vigorously in support of women who wished to make a career for themselves. Her views might not have altogether pleased her mother, the truest Victorian of them all, but like her sisters, she was not afraid to take issue with 'Dearest Mama's' way of thinking. She could also count herself more fortunate than her two elder sisters who both married German princes and found themselves in a land where prejudice against women was even more deeply entrenched into the national character than in England. She may be one of the less well-remembered princesses of the era, but in her way she proved herself a worthy and well-respected member of the family, laying down a blueprint which other princesses from later generations were pleased to follow.

Portraits of Princess Helena

The Royal Collection includes several portraits of Helena, all of which are listed online and most with accompanying images. The majority of them, some being of groups of some or all of the family, were painted during her childhood. Those of her in adult life include pictures by Franz Xaver Winterhalter (1861 and 1865), William Corden the Younger (1864), Albert Graefle (1864), painted for her as a birthday portrait from the Queen, and Heinrich von Angeli (1875). The official portrait of her wedding ceremony in 1866 is by Christian Karl Magnussen.

There is also a portrait of Prince Christian by Winterhalter (1866), and, it might be noted, also one of a shorthorn heifer named Princess Helena at the farm on Windsor by Friedrich Wilhelm Keyl.

The National Portrait Gallery, London, has a portrait of Princesses Helena and Louise and Prince Arthur, 'Opening of the Royal Albert Infirmary at Bishop's Waltham' (1865), the work of an unknown artist [see p.18].

Queen Victoria and Prince Albert, 1854

Queen Victoria, Prince Albert and their children, 1857, l to r: Princess Alice; Prince Arthur; the Prince of Wales; Prince Leopold; Princess Louise; Princess Beatrice (on mother's lap); Prince Alfred; the Princess Royal; Princess Helena

Princesses Helena and Louise, 1856

A photomontage of Queen Victoria, the Prince Consort and their children, with Princess Helena on the right

Princess Helena, c.1864

Princesses Alice, Louise, Beatrice, Victoria (Princess Royal and Crown Princess of Prussia) and Helena in mourning around a bust of the Prince Consort, 1862

Princess Helena and Prince Christian of Schleswig-Holstein at the time of their engagement

Princess Helena and Prince Christian of Schleswig-Holstein at the time of their engagement

Princess Helena and Prince Christian of Schleswig-Holstein on their wedding day, 5 July 1866

Princess Helena, c.1875

Prince Christian, c.1890

Prince Christian Victor, c.1897

Princess Helena, c.1905

A statue of Prince Christian Victor, outside the north gate, Windsor Castle

Princess Helena, c.1909

Princess Helena, 1911

Princess Marie Louise, c.1912

Prince Aribert of Anhalt

Prince Albert of Schleswig-Holstein, c.1920

Princess Marie Valerie of Schleswig-Holstein

Princess Helena Victoria, c.1920

Reference Notes

PH – Princess Helena
QV – Queen Victoria
CPFW - Crown Princess Frederick William
EF – Empress Frederick

Foreword

1 Epton, 234

Chapter 1

1 *Letters of the Prince Consort,* Prince Albert to King Frederick William IV, 26.5.1846, 103-4
2 *The Prince Consort and his brother*, Prince Albert to Duke Ernest, 26.5.1846, 86-7
3 Queen Victoria's Journal, 12.6.1846
4 *Letters of Lady Augusta Stanley*, 20.9.1849 (?), 38
5 *Letters of Queen Victoria, 1837-1861,* Vol II, 220, 22.5.1849
6 Eagle, 'For dearest Mama and Papa'
7 Bennett, *Queen Victoria's Children,* 89-90
8 Weintraub, *Albert*, 302
9 *Letters of Lady Augusta Stanley*, 3.9.1852, 39
10 ibid, 17.9.1856, 97
11 Victoria, Queen, *Dearest Child*, 175, QV to Princess Victoria, 9.4.1859
12 ibid. 141, QV to Princess Victoria, 27.10.1858
13 ibid. 139, QV to Princess Victoria, 18.10.1858
14 Baird, 69, PH to Emily Maude, 28.3.1861
15 Noel, 55, Prince of Wales to Princess Alice, 17.8.1860
16 Victoria, Queen, *Dearest Child*, 353, QV to CPFW, 1.10.1861
17 Wake, 42
18 *Letters of Lady Augusta Stanley*, 19.12.1861, 245
19 Dennison, 26
20 Baird, 75-6, PH to Emily Maude, 20.1.1862

21 Victoria, Queen, *Dearest Mama*, 53, QV to CPFW, 16.4.1862
22 Baird, 79, PH to Emily Baird, 19.4.1862
23 Zeepvat, 34, PH to Leopold, 3.5.1862
24 Victoria, Queen, *Dearest Mama*, 100, QV to CPFW, 12.8.1862
25 Baird, 81, PH to Emily Maude, 22.7.1862
26 Victoria, Queen, *Dearest Mama*, 127, QV to CPFW, 8.11.1862
27, 28 Maas, 69-71
29 Chomet, 15
30 *Royalty Digest*, April 2000, 315 and June 2000, 374
31 Victoria, Queen, *Dearest Mama*, 198, QV to CPFW, 18.4.1863
32 ibid, 311, QV to CPFW, 23.3.1864
33 ibid, 314, QV to CPFW, 26.3.1864
34 Corti, 145
35 *Letters of Lady Augusta Stanley*, 315-6, 11.11.1863

Chapter 2

1 *Letters of Queen Victoria, 1862-1885,* Vol I, 89, 18.5.1863, QV to King Leopold
2 Victoria, Queen, *Your Dear Letter*, 27, QV to CPFW, 23.5.1865
3 Grey, 9-10
4 Madol, 174
5 Battiscombe, 76
6 *Letters of the Empress Frederick*, 57, CPFW to QV, 18.4.1865
7 *Letters of Queen Victoria, 1862-1885,* Vol I, 272, 24.8.1865, QV to King Leopold
8 Victoria, Queen, *Your Dear Letter*, 42, QV to CPFW, 11.9.1865
9 Victoria, Queen, *Further Letters,* 157-8, QV to Queen Augusta, 17.10.1865
10 Battiscombe, 76
11 Longford, 369
12, 13 Battiscombe, 76
14 Weintraub, *Victoria,* 375
15 Victoria, Queen, *Your Dear Letter*, 42, QV to CPFW, 11.9.1865
16 ibid, 43, QV to CPFW, 26.9.1865
17 Noel, 120, QV to King Leopold, 4.10.1865
18 Battiscombe, 77
19 ibid, 78
20 Victoria, Queen, *Your Dear Letter*, 56-7, QV to CPFW, 24.1.1866
21 ibid 57, QV to CPFW, 31.1.1866
22 St Aubyn, *Queen Victoria*, 412
23 St Aubyn, *Edward*, 100
24 *The Times,* 7.2.1866
25 Chomet, 54
26 Baird, 94, PH to Emily Maude, 26.5.1866
27 *Dundee Courier & Argus*, 12.5.1866

28 Victoria, Queen, *Your Dear Letter*, 82, QV to CPFW, 28.7.1866
29 *Later Letters of Lady Augusta Stanley,* 51
30 Chomet, 47
31 Victoria, Queen, *Your Dear Letter*, 59, QV to CPFW, 9.3.1866
32, 33 *The Times*, 6.7.1866
34 Chomet, 49
35 Victoria, Queen, *Your Dear Letter*, 78, QV to CPFW, 7.7.1866
36 ibid, 81, QV to CPFW, 18.7.1866

Chapter 3

1 Baird, 96, PH to Emily Maude, 9.9.1866
2 Wake, 65
3 Baird, 114, PH to Emily Baird, 14.9.1872
4 Longford, 168, Prince Leopold to Princess Louise, 22.8.1872
5 *Later Letters of Lady Augusta Stanley,* 76
6 QV's Journal, 10.12.1873
7 Anon, 'Silver wedding eulogy for Prince and Princess Christian'
8 Epton, 151
9 RA. Add c/20/11, Sir Francis Seymour to his wife Agnes, 28.11.1874
10 Chomet, 73, PH to Sir Theodore Martin, 16.2.1884
11 Victoria, Queen, *Your Dear Letter*, 115, QV to CPFW, 15.1.1867
12 ibid, 197, QV to CPFW, 27.6.1868
13 Victoria, Queen, *Darling Child*, 4, QV to CPFW, 6.5.1871
14 ibid, 44, QV to CPFW, 1.12.1872
15 Longford, 163, QV to Louise, 26.1.1872
16 Victoria, Queen, *Your Dear Letter*, 289, QV to CPFW, 1.8.1870
17 Victoria, Queen, *Darling Child*, 70, QV to CPFW, 1.12.1872
18 ibid, 112-3, QV to CPFW, 20.10.1873
19 Poore, 16
20 ibid, 45
21 Marie Louise, 20
22 ibid, 32
23 Chomet, 55
24 Marie Louise, 32
25 Chomet, 56
26 Marie Louise, 32
27 Chomet, 118
28 Queen Victoria's Journal, 12/14/20.5.1876
29 ibid, 7.5.1877

Chapter 4

1 Corti, 242

2 Battiscombe, 233
3 Epton, 232
4 Marie Louise, 18
5 Hall, 210
6 Hudson 115
7 Hudson, 116; Cooper, 59-60
8 Röhl, *Kaiser's early life,* 333, CPFW to Crown Prince Frederick William, 23.9.1878
9 Pakula, 369-70, PH to CPFW, 16.9.1879
10 Victoria, Queen, *Beloved Mama,* 110, QV to CPFW, 12.11.1881
11 Zeepvat, 156, QV to CPFW, 13.1.1881
12 Alice (1884), [9-10]
13 ibid, 152, QV to CPFW, 5.12.1883
14 Chomet, 84
15 Röhl, *Kaiser's early life,* 642
16 Corti, 337; Röhl, *Kaiser's early life,* 644
17 Chomet, 78
18 Pakula, 355
19 *The Times,* 20.9.1887
20 Chomet, 76
21 Poore, 57
22 ibid, 60
23 *The Times,* 14.2.1888
24 ibid, 11.7.1888
25 Reid, 265
26 Röhl, *Kaiser's personal monarchy,* 62
27 *Letters of the Empress Frederick,* 328, PH to Lady Ponsonby, 4 August 1888
28 Victoria, *The Empress Frederick writes to Sophie,* 73, EF to Princess Sophie, December 1890

Chapter 5

1 Baird, 116, PH to Emily Baird, 19.3.1891
2 Pope-Hennessy, 216, QV to EF, 16.12.1891
3 ibid, 252, Princess of Wales to Prince George, autumn 1892
4 Queen Victoria's Journal, 26.12.1891
5 Reid, 117
6 QV to Prince Christian Victor, 8.1.1892 (previously unpublished letter, private collection)
7 Baird, 117-8, PH to Emily Baird, 13.2.1892
8 Chomet, 60
9 Hall, 33, PH to Sir Henry Ponsonby
10 ibid, 30-1, PH to Miss Huxley, 31.3.1893
11 *The Times,* 7.5.1887
12 ibid, 12.12.1895

13 ibid, 6.6.1896
14 Poore, 148
15 Helena, Princess, 'Trained Nurses and Nursing in England'; Chomet, 153
16 Lytton, 24, diary 4.10.1895
17 Mallet, Marie Mallet to Bernard Mallet, 24.1.1891, 40
18 ibid, Marie Mallet to Bernard Mallet, 5.4.1891, 50
19 Wake, 320
20 Marie Mallet diary 18.6.96, Wake, 320
21 Reid, 103
22 Dennison, 193, PH to Professor Story, 29.1.1896
23 Reid, 106
24 ibid, 25
25 Poore, 169
26 Victoria, *The Empress Frederick writes to Sophie,* 312, EF to Princess Sophie, autumn 1899
27 Chomet, 105
28 *Letters of Queen Victoria, 1886-1901,* Vol III, 578-9, Queen's Journal 27.7-31.7.1900
29 ibid, 614, Queen's Journal 27.10.1900
30 Victoria, *The Empress Frederick writes to Sophie,* 337-8, EF to Princess Sophie, November 1900
31 Victoria, Queen, *Beloved and Darling Child,* 257, QV to EF, 30.10.1900
32 Mallet, 220, Marie Mallet to Bernard Mallet, 16.11.1900
33 Poore, 280
34 Marie Louise, 112
35 Röhl, *Kaiser's personal monarchy,* 663-4
36 Chomet, 65-6
37 Packard, 319
38 Victoria, Queen, *Beloved and Darling Child,* 258, QV to EF, 27.12.1900

Chapter 6

1 *Letters of Queen Victoria, 1886-1901,* Vol III, 642, Queen's Journal 13.1.1901
2 Gore, 140
3 Wake, 340
4 Reid, 206
5 Poore, 268
6 Baird, 121, PH to Emily Baird, 8.4.1901
7 ibid, 122, PH to Emily Baird, 25.5.1901
8 Victoria, *The Empress Frederick writes to Sophie,* 346, EF to Princess Sophie, summer 1901
9 Ridley, 358-9, PH to King Edward VII, 6.8.1901
10 Poore, 272
11 Marie Louise, 124
12 Poore, 284

13 Marie Louise, 250-1
14 Poore, 318
15, 16 Hudson, 127
17 Poore, 320

Chapter 7

1 *The Times*, 14.3.1913
2 ibid, 29.1.1914
3 Wake, 388
4 Chomet, 130
5 Poore, 325
6, 7 Wake, 396, PH to Lady Augusta Montagu, 20.8.1914
8 Hudson, 131-2
9 Marie Louise, 17-8
10 ibid, 179-80
11 Hall, 38, PH to Miss Isobel Macdonald, 6.7.1917
12 ibid, 38, PH to Mrs Fenwick, 15.3.1918
13 ibid, 39, PH to Miss Macdonald, 18.4.1918
14 ibid, 39, PH to Miss Macdonald, 24.4.1918
15 Baird, 135, PH to Emily Baird, 6.11.1917
16 *The Times*, 5.11.1917
17 ibid, 136, PH to Emily Baird, 29.10.1918

Chapter 8

1 Chomet, 144
2 Edwards, 274-5
3 Poore, 349
4 *The Times*, 10.11.1921
5 Chomet, 146-7
6 *The Times*, 8.2.1923
7 ibid, 14.2.1923
8 Baird, 140-1, Emily Loch to Emily Baird, 25.5.1923
9 *The Times*, various references, 31.5.1923-5.6.1923
10 ibid, 13.6.1923
11 ibid, 16.6.1923
12 Baird, 141, Emily Loch to Emily Baird, 17.6.1923
13 *Windsor, Slough & Eton Express*, 19.12.1924
14 Hall, 39-40
15 The Times, 11.6.1923

Bibliography

Books

The place of publication is London unless otherwise stated

Albert, Prince Consort, *Letters of the Prince Consort, 1831-1861;* sel. and ed. Kurt Jagow, John Murray, 1938

Alice, Grand Duchess of Hesse, *Biographical sketch and letters,* John Murray, 1884

Battiscombe, Georgina, *Queen Alexandra*, Constable, 1969

Bennett, Daphne, *King without a crown: Albert, Prince Consort of England, 1819-1861,* Heinemann, 1977

-- *Queen Victoria's children,* Victor Gollancz, 1980

-- *Vicky, Princess Royal of England and German Empress,* Collins Harvill, 1971

Benson, E.F., *Daughters of Queen Victoria,* Cassell, 1939

Bolitho, Hector, ed., *The Prince Consort and his brother: two hundred new letters,* Cobden-Sanderson, 1933

Chomet, Seweryn, *Helena: A princess reclaimed,* New York, Begell House, 1999

Cooper, C.W., *Town and country,* Lovat-Dickinson, 1937

Corti, Count Egon, *The downfall of three dynasties,* Methuen, 1934

Croft, Christina, *Queen Victoria's granddaughters, 1860-1918,* Hilliard & Croft, 2013

Cullen, Tom, *The Empress Brown: The story of a royal friendship,* Bodley Head, 1969

Dennison, Matthew, *The last princess: The devoted life of Queen Victoria's youngest daughter,* Weidenfeld & Nicolson, 2007

Duff, David, *The shy princess: The life of HRH Princess Beatrice, the youngest daughter and constant companion of Queen Victoria,* Evans, 1958; Frederick Muller, 1974

Edwards, Anne, *Matriarch: Queen Mary and the house of Windsor,* Hodder & Stoughton, 1984

Epton, Nina, *Victoria and her daughters,* Weidenfeld & Nicolson, 1971

Gore, John, *King George V: A personal memoir,* John Murray, 1941

Grey, Charles [uncredited on cover and title page], *The early years of the Prince Consort:* compiled for and annotated by Queen Victoria, William Kimber, 1967

Hall, Coryne, *Princesses on the wards: Royal women in nursing through wars and revolutions,* Stroud: History Press, 2014

Hough, Richard, *Louis and Victoria: The first Mountbattens,* Hutchinson, 1974

Hudson, Helen, *Cumberland Lodge: A house through history,* Chichester: Phillimore, 1997

Kennedy, A.L. ed., *'My dear Duchess': Social and political letters to the Duchess of Manchester 1858-1869,* John Murray, 1956

Longford, Elizabeth, (ed.) *Darling Loosy: Letters to Princess Louise 1856-1939,* Weidenfeld & Nicolson, 1991

Lytton, Lady, *Lady Lytton's Court Diary 1895-1899,* Rupert Hart-Davis, 1961

Madol, Hans Roger, *Christian IX,* Collins, 1939

Mallet, Victor, ed., *Life with Queen Victoria: Marie Mallet's letters from court, 1887-1901,* John Murray, 1968

Marie Louise, Princess, *My memories of six reigns,* Evans Bros, 1956

Mullen, Richard, & Munson, James, *Victoria: Portrait of a Queen,* BBC, 1987

Noel, Gerard, *Princess Alice: Queen Victoria's forgotten daughter,* Constable, 1974

Oxford Dictionary of National Biography

Packard, Jerrold, *Farewell in splendour: The death of Queen Victoria and her age,* Sutton, 2000

-- *Victoria's daughters,* New York: St Martin's Press, 1998; Stroud: Sutton, 1999

Pakula, Hannah, *An uncommon woman: The Empress Frederick,* Weidenfeld & Nicolson, 1996

Poore, Judith U., *The memoirs of Emily Loch, Discretion in waiting: Tsarina Alexandra and the Christian family,* Kinloss, Librario, 2007

Pope-Hennessy, James, *Queen Mary, 1867-1953,* Allen & Unwin, 1959

Reid, Michaela, *Ask Sir James: Sir James Reid, Personal Physician to Queen Victoria and physician-in-ordinary to three monarchs,* Hodder & Stoughton, 1987

Rennell, Tony, *Last days of glory: The death of Queen Victoria,* Viking, 2000

Ridley, Jane, *Bertie: A life of Edward VII,* Chatto & Windus, 2012

Röhl, John, *Wilhelm II: The Kaiser's personal monarchy, 1888-1900,* Cambridge University Press, 2004

-- *Wilhelm II: Into the abyss of war and exile, 1900-1941,* Cambridge University Press, 2014
-- *Young Wilhelm: The Kaiser's early life, 1859-1888,* Cambridge University Press, 1998
St Aubyn, Giles, *Edward VII, Prince and King,* Collins, 1979
-- *Queen Victoria: a portrait,* Sinclair-Stevenson, 1991
Stanley, Lady Augusta, *Letters of Lady Augusta Stanley, A young lady at court, 1849-1863;* ed. Dean of Windsor & Hector Bolitho, Gerald Howe, 1927
-- *Later letters of Lady Augusta Stanley, 1864-1876;* ed. Dean of Windsor & Hector Bolitho, Jonathan Cape, 1929
Van der Kiste, John, *Queen Victoria's daughters,* Sutton, 1986, rev. History Press, 2009
Victoria, Consort of Frederick III, German Emperor, *The Empress Frederick writes to Sophie,* Faber, 1955
-- *Letters of the Empress Frederick,* ed. Sir Frederick Ponsonby, Macmillan, 1928
Victoria, Queen, *The Letters of Queen Victoria: a Selection from Her Majesty's Correspondence between the years 1837 and 1861,* ed. A.C. Benson & Viscount Esher, 3 vols, John Murray, 1907
-- *The Letters of Queen Victoria, 2nd Series: a Selection from Her Majesty's Correspondence and Journal between the years 1862 and 1885,* ed. G. E. Buckle, 3 vols, John Murray, 1926-8
-- *The Letters of Queen Victoria, 3rd Series: a Selection from Her Majesty's Correspondence and Journal between the years 1886 and 1901,* ed. G.E. Buckle, 3 vols, John Murray, 1930-2
-- *Further Letters of Queen Victoria, from the Archives of the House of Brandenburg-Prussia;* ed. Hector Bolitho, Thornton Butterworth, 1938
-- *Dearest Child: Letters between Queen Victoria and the Princess Royal, 1858-1861;* ed. Roger Fulford, Evans Bros, 1964
-- *Dearest Mama: Private Correspondence of Queen Victoria and the Crown Princess of Prussia, 1861-1864;* ed. Roger Fulford, Evans Bros, 1968
-- *Your Dear Letter: Private Correspondence of Queen Victoria and the Crown Princess of Prussia, 1865-1871,* ed. Roger Fulford, Evans Bros, 1971
-- *Darling Child: Private Correspondence of Queen Victoria and the Crown Princess of Prussia, 1871-1878;* ed. Roger Fulford, Evans Bros, 1976

-- *Beloved Mama: Private Correspondence of Queen Victoria and the German Crown Princess of Prussia, 1878-1885;* ed. Roger Fulford, Evans Bros, 1981
-- *Beloved and Darling Child: Last letters Queen Victoria and her eldest daughter, 1886-1901;* ed. Agatha Ramm, Stroud, Sutton, 1990
-- *Advice to a grand-daughter: Letters from Queen Victoria to Princess Victoria of Hesse,* ed. Richard Hough, Heinemann, 1975
Vovk, Justin C., *Imperial requiem: Four royal women and the fall of the age of empires,* Bloomington, iUniverse, 2012
Wake, Jehanne, *Princess Louise: Queen Victoria's unconventional daughter,* Collins, 1988
Wallis, Nevile, ed., *A Victorian canvas: The memoirs of W.P. Frith, R.A.,* Geoffrey Bles, 1957
Warren, T. Herbert, *Prince Christian Victor: The story of a young soldier,* John Murray, 1903
Weintraub, Stanley, *The importance of being Edward: King in waiting 1841-1901,* John Murray, 2000
-- *Victoria: Biography of a Queen,* Unwin Hyman, 1987
Woodham-Smith, Mrs Cecil, *Queen Victoria, her life and times, Vol. 1, 1819-1861,* Hamish Hamilton, 1972
Zeepvat, Charlotte, *Prince Leopold: The untold story of Queen Victoria's youngest son,* Stroud, Sutton, 1998

Journals

Dundee Courier & Argus
The Times
Royalty Digest
Windsor, Eton & Slough Express

Articles

Anon., 'Silver wedding eulogy for Prince and Princess Christian'. In *The Graphic*, 1891, reprinted in *Royalty Digest*, January 1999
Eagle, Judith, 'For dearest Mama and Papa: Queen Victoria's children as artists'. In *Country Life*, 8 September 1977

Helena, Princess (Princess Christian), 'Trained Nurses and Nursing in England'. In *Woman and Home*, 1895, reprinted in Chomet, *Helena: a princess reclaimed*

Spencer-Warren, M., 'The Prince and Princess Christian'. In *The Strand Magazine*, July-December 1895

Zeepvat, Charlotte, 'She is wanting in charm'. In *Royalty Digest*, March 1994

Online

Queen Victoria's Journal, www.queenvictoriasjournals.org, accessed February 2015

The Royal Collection, www.royalcollection.org.uk/collection, accessed February 2015 (*see p.101*)

Index

C - Prince Christian of Schleswig-Holstein
H – Helena, Princess Christian of Schleswig-Holstein
QV – Queen Victoria

Kings and Queens are of England unless stated otherwise

Addison, Christopher (1869-1951), 88
Adolf of Schaumburg-Lippe, Prince (1859-1916), 59-60
Albert of Saxe-Coburg Gotha, Prince Consort of England (1819-61), 6, 14-5, 19, 21-2, 29, 32, 35, 49, 57, 86; and birth of H, 5; death, 10-1; H translates letters for biography of, 17-8
Albert of Schleswig-Holstein, Prince (1869-1931), 45, 62, 74; birth, 32, 35; education, 39; and Marie Valerie, 75-6; as heir to family duchy, and fighting during First World War, 90-1
Albert Victor, Duke of Clarence (1864-92), 61
Albrecht of Prussia, Prince (1837-1906), 18
Alexander II, Tsar of Russia (1818-81), 43
Alexander III, Tsar of Russia (1845-94), 51
Alexander John of Wales, Prince (b. & d. 1871), 41
Alexander of Battenberg, Prince of Bulgaria, later Count von Hartenau (1857-93), 43, 50-1, 59
Alexander of Hesse, Prince (1823-88), 16
Alexandra, Queen (1844-1925), 13, 21, 34, 41, 82, 99; and H's marriage, 24; opposes idea of one of H's daughters marrying one of her sons, 61; and relations with H and C, 80
Alexandra (Alix), Empress of Russia (1872-1918), 97
Alfred, Duke of Edinburgh, later Duke of Saxe-Coburg Gotha (1844-1900), 6-8, 10, 19, 43, 48; reconciles Prince of Wales to H's marriage, 25; death, 73-4
Alice, Countess of Athlone (1883-1981), 44
Alice, Grand Duchess of Hesse and the Rhine (1843-78), 6-11, 17-8, 35, 43, 52; wedding, 12-3; and H's marriage, 23-4; letters edited by H, 48-9; death, 53
Angeli, Heinrich von (1840-1925), 103
Argyll, John Campbell, 9th Duke of (1845-1914), 35, 89
Aribert of Anhalt, Prince (1866-1933), 60-1, 75, 92
Arthur, Duke of Connaught and Strathearn (1850-1942), 12, 18, 29, 56, 80, 90, 103; and C's shooting accident, 62-3

Asquith, Herbert Henry (1852-1928), 90-1
Augusta Victoria, German Empress (1858-1921), 46-7
Augusta, Duchess of Cambridge (1797-1889), 5, 23, 29
Augusta, German Empress (1811-90), 18, 21-3, 52, 57
Augusta, Princess (1768-1840), 31, 40

Baird, Emily *see* Emily Maude
Balhausen, Lucius von (1835-1914), 51
Beatrice, Princess (1857-1944), 8, 12-3, 15, 23, 28-9, 32, 36, 40, 70, 73, 82, 85-6, 98, 100; QV relies on in last years, 67-8, 76-7; at QV's deathbed and funeral, 78-9
Bergsträsser, Dr Arnold, 48-50
Bigge, Sir Arthur and Lady *see* Stamfordham
Bismarck, Herbert von (1849-1904), 51
Bismarck, Otto von (1815-98), 19, 23, 28, 50
Blücher, Countess, 22
Botha, Louis, 84
Bourdillon, F.W., 34
Bowater, Louisa, 29
Bradford, Selina, Countess of (d.1894), 38
Bridgeman, William, 99
Brown, John (1826-83), 9, 24
Bruce, Lady Augusta, later Lady Augusta Stanley (1821-76), 6, 8, 11, 16, 22, 27, 34
Buckland, Frank, 33
Butt, Clara, 39

Campbell, Lady Muriel, 29
Carnegie, Andrew, 82
Carol I, King of Roumania (1839-1914), 60
Caroline Matilda, Duchess of Schleswig-Holstein (1860-1932), 46-8
Castlerosse, Lord, 28
Charles, Duke of Albany and Duke of Saxe-Coburg Gotha (1884-1954), 48
Charlotte, Queen (1744-1818), 31, 49, 92
Chesterfield, Anne, Countess of, 38
Christian IX, King of Denmark (1818-1906), 15, 18-9, 24
Christian of Schleswig-Holstein, Prince (1831-1917), 47-8, 50, 53-4, 59, 61, 66, 69-70, 75-6, 80-1, 83, 90-1, 96; birth, 20; character and interests, 20, 22, 32-4, 36, 39; plans for marriage, 19, 21-5; wedding, 25-9; honeymoon, 29-30; at Frogmore, 30; at Cumberland Lodge, 31, 44-5; and upbringing of children, 34; and Franco-Prussian war, 36; and stillborn son, 41-2; QV's financial provision for, 45-6; and marriage of Marie Louise, 60; silver wedding anniversary, 60; shooting accident and loss of eye, 62-3; and H's ill-health, 71; and QV's diamond jubilee, 71; and Christian Victor's death, 74; and QV's death, 78; No 78 Pall Mall left to, 79; represents Edward VII at foreign

functions, 85; increasing ill-health, 86-7; golden wedding anniversary, 92; and change of family name, 94; death and funeral, 94

Christian Victor Schleswig-Holstein, Prince (1867-1900), 60, 62, 83, 85, 100; birth, 32; education, 39; sporting activities, 45; persuades H to take up photography, 71; and Boer War, 72-3; death, 74

Churchill, Lady Jane (1826-1900), 76

Clynes, J.R. (1869-1949), 100

Constantine, King of Greece (1868-1923), 58

Corden, William, the Younger (1819-1900), 103

Cowans, Sir John (1862-1921), 92

Dalou, Aimee-Jules (1838-1902), 42

Dawson, Bertrand, Viscount Dawson of Penn (1864-1945) 99

Dickens, Charles (1812-70), 54

Disraeli, Benjamin, Earl of Beaconsfield (1804-81), 34, 38

Edgcumbe, Lady Ernestine, 29

Edmonstone, Lady, 98

Edward of Saxe-Weimar, Prince (1823-1902), 28

Edward VII, King (1841-1910), 6, 8-9, 11, 13-5, 34, 36, 47, 51, 82; and H's marriage, 25, 27, 29; and QV's death, 77-8; and relations with H and C, 80; death, 85

Elizabeth, Queen, formerly Lady Elizabeth Bowes-Lyon (1900-2002), 98

Engelbert-Charles, Duke of Arenberg (1899-1974), 75

Ernest, Duke of Saxe-Coburg Gotha (1818-93), 5, 27, 73

Ernest, Grand Duke of Hesse and the Rhine (1868-1937), 62, 70

Ernest Gunther, Duke of Schleswig-Holstein (1863-1921), 90

Esmarch, Friedrich von (1823-1908), 45

Fairbank, Dr, 40

Faucit, Helena, 18

Fenwick, Mrs Bedford, 55, 93-4

Ferdinand of Portugal, Prince (1846-61), 10

Ferdinand, King of Roumania (1865-1927), 60

Fitzwilliam, Lady Mary, 29

Francis Ferdinand, Archduke of Austria-Hungary (1863-1914), 90

Francis, Duke of Teck (1837-1900), 61

Frederick Charles, Landgrave of Hesse-Cassel (1868-1940), 66

Frederick II, King of Prussia ('the Great') (1712-86), 52, 58

Frederick III, Emperor, formerly Frederick William, Crown Prince of Prussia and Germany (1831-88), 20, 23, 27, 56; wedding, 9; illness and death, 55

Frederick Louis, Prince of Wales (1707-51), 21

Frederick V, King of Denmark (1723-66), 21

Frederick VII, King of Denmark (1808-63), 19

Frederick, Duke of Schleswig-Holstein (1829-80), 19, 24, 28, 46-8

Frederick William IV, King of Prussia (1795-1861), 5

Friedberg, Heinrich von (1813-95), 56-7
Frith, William Powell (1819-1909), 13-4
Fullerton, Sir John, 83

George I, King of Greece (1845-1913), 19
George II, King (1683-1760), 21
George III, King (1738-1820), 21-2, 31, 40, 92
George V, King (1865-1936), 61, 77, 80, 83, 85-7, 90, 92, 96, 98-101; and change of family name, 94
George VI, King, formerly Albert, Duke of York (1895-1952), 98
George, Duke of Cambridge (1819-1904), 23, 28
George, Grand Duke of Mecklenburg-Strelitz (1779-1860), 5
Gladstone, William Ewart (1809-98), 34, 54, 87
Glyn, Ralph and Mary, 89
Goldschmidt, Otto, 39
Gordon Lennox, Lady Caroline, 29
Graefle, Albert (1809-89), 103
Grant Duff, Sir M.E., 52
Grey, Charles (1804-70), 17-8, 25-6, 30

Hamilton, Lady Albertha, 29
Hamilton, William, 6
Harald, Prince (b. & d. 1876), 41
Helen, Duchess of Albany (1861-1922), 48, 82
Helena, Princess, birth and christening, 5-6; character, 6-10, 16, 22, 37, 44; and death of Prince Consort, 11; confirmation, 11-2; as eldest daughter left at home, 12-3, 15; and W.P. Frith, 13-4; and Carl Ruland, 14-5; eighteenth birthday, 17; translates letters of Prince Consort for biography, 17-8; plans for marriage, betrothal, and wedding, 18-29; honeymoon, 30-1; at Frogmore, 31; birth and upbringing of children, 32, 34, 39; at Cumberland Lodge, 32, 45-6, 86-7; depression, 32, 42, 71; ill-health, 35, 37-8, 53-4, 57, 68-9, 71, 98; and relations with Alice, 35; and Franco-Prussian war, 36; charity work, 36, 40, 43-5, 54-5, 63-6, 82-3, 86, 88-9, 91-3, 97-8; musical interests, 39; and birth and death of Harald, 40; and stillborn son, 41; QV's financial provision for, 45-6; and Emperor William II, 46-7, 56-8, 91; and question of marriage between Leopold and Caroline Matilda of Schleswig-Holstein, 47-8; and publication of Alice's letters, 48-50; 1887 visit to Berlin, 50-1; publication of memoirs of Wilhelmina, Margravine of Bayreuth, 51-3; anxiety about eyesight, 54, 70; in Germany after death of Emperor Frederick III, 55-8; and marriage of Marie Louise, 60; silver wedding anniversary, 60; apparent unpleasantness to family, 61; and C's eye accident, 62-3; QV relies on in last years, 67-76; with QV and Beatrice at Cimiez, 70; and Dr Reid, 70-1; and QV's diamond jubilee, 71-2; and death of Alfred, 73; and death of Christian Victor, 73-4; at QV's deathbed and funeral procession, 80-1; No 78 Pall Mall left to, 79; final visit to Empress Frederick and her funeral, 79-80; relations with Edward VII, 80; visits Africa, 83-5; and death of Edward VII, 85; at

coronation of George V, 86; sympathy with women's suffrage, 87; granted Cumberland Lodge for life, 87; and death of Duke of Argyll, 89; and World War I, 90, 97; golden wedding anniversary, 92; and change of family name, 94; and death of C, 94-5; problems with commissioners over residence, 96; death, funeral and tributes, 99-101; portraits of, 103

Helena Victoria, Princess (1870-1948), 53, 66, 74-5, 79, 81, 83, 87, 94, 99, 101; birth, 32; and possibility of engagement to George of Wales, 61-2

Hélène, Princess d'Orléans, 5

Henry of Battenberg, Prince (1858-96), 16, 62, 68, 70, 73

Henry of Hesse, Prince, 18

Hocédé, Mme, 15

Hoffmeister, Dr, 62

Horn, Dr Georg, 53

Humbert I, King of Italy (1844-1900), 73

Keyl, Friedrich Wilhelm (1823-71), 103

Lawson, George, 62

Leopold I, King of the Belgians (1790-1865). 17. 19-21, 24

Leopold II, King of the Belgians (1835-1909), 79

Leopold, Duke of Albany (1853-84), 29, 32, 47-8

Liddell, Captain, 96

Lind, Jenny, 39

Lloyd-Lindsay, Robert, later Baron Wantage, 36

Loch, Alice, 49

Loch, Emily, 37, 49, 54, 66, 69-71, 74-5, 79, 81, 86, 90, 97, 99, 101

Louis, Grand Duke of Hesse and the Rhine (1837-92), 10, 12, 17-8, 53

Louis of Battenberg, Prince (1852-1921), 16

Louise, Duchess of Argyll (1848-1939), 6, 8-9, 12-6, 18, 23, 28-9, 32, 35-6, 42, 52, 61, 68, 71, 80, 82, 86, 100, 103; QV relies on in last years, 67; at QV's deathbed and funeral procession, 78-9; and Duke of Argyll's death, 89

Louise, Duchess of Fife and Princess Royal (1867-1931), 85-6

Louise, Queen of Denmark (1817-98), 19

Lytton, Lady Edith Villiers Bulwer-Lytton (1841-1936), 67

Macdonald, Isabel, 92-3

Mackenzie, Dr Morell (1837-92), 55-6

Magnussen, Christian Karl, 103

Mallet, Marie (1861-1934), 67-8, 74

Margaret, Landgravine of Hesse-Cassel (1872-1954), 66

Margaret, Crown Princess of Sweden (1882-1920), 92

Marie Feodorovna, Dowager Empress of Russia (1847-1928), 99

Marie Louise, Princess (1872-1957), 37-9, 43, 53, 74, 76, 84, 92, 94, 97; birth, 32; engagement and wedding, 60-1; breakdown of marriage, 75

Marie, Duchess of Edinburgh (1853-1920), 43, 48

Martin, Sir Theodore, 34, 49

Marx, Karl, 52
Mary Adelaide, Duchess of Teck (1833-97), 36, 61
Mary, Queen (1867-1953), 61, 86-7, 89, 92, 99
Maude, Emily, later Emily Baird, 9, 11-3, 26, 31-2, 60, 63, 81, 94-5, 98, 101
Maude, George, 9
Minto, Gilbert, Earl of (1845-1914), 75
Montagu, Lady Augusta, 90
Moore, H.O., 94
Morris, William, 44
Murray, John, 50
Murray, Lady Alexandrina, 29

Nicholas II, Tsar of Russia (1868-1918), 97
Nightingale, Florence (1820-1910), 39, 43, 55, 64, 66, 99

Oldenburg, Elimar, Duke of (1844-95), 18
Olga, Queen of the Hellenes (1851-1926), 98

Pagenstecher, Dr Herman, 54, 70
Paget, Sir Augustus (1823-96), 18
Paget, Sir James, 56
Palmerston, Henry John Temple, Viscount (1784-1865), 19
Pedro V, King of Portugal (1837-61), 10
Phipps, Lady Laura, 29
Plymouth, Robert George Windsor-Clive, Earl of (1857-1923), 86
Ponsonby, Mary, Lady (1832-1916), 57
Ponsonby, Sir Frederick, 1st Baron Sysonby (1867-1935), 96
Ponsonby, Sir Henry (1825-95), 33, 63, 68

Reid, Sir James (1849-1923), 54, 56, 62, 67-71, 77-9
Reid, Susan 78
Reischach, Hugo von, 58
Roberts, Frederick, Earl (1832-1914), 73
Rudolf, Crown Prince of Austria-Hungary (1858-89), 50-1
Ruland, Carl (1834-1907), 14-5, 52

Sahl, Hermann, 49
Schwalb, Anna and Rubin, 75
Scott, Lady Margaret, 29
Sell, Karl, 48-50
Seymour, Sir Francis, 33
Sigismund of Prussia, Prince (1864-6), 27
Smuts, Jan, 84
Somerset, Lady Geraldine, 23
Sophie, Countess Chotek, Duchess of Hohenberg (1868-1914), 90
Sophie, Queen of Greece (1870-1932), 58, 66, 72, 74, 81

Stamfordham, Sir Arthur, Baron (1849-1931), formerly Sir Arthur Bigge, and Lady S, 68, 88
Stanley, Arthur, Dean of Westminster (1815-81) 16
Stanley, Lady Augusta, *see* Bruce
Stockmar, Christian, Baron (1787-1863), 14
Strauss, David Friedrich, 52
Stott, David, 52
Sutherland, Duchess of, 36
Sydney, Lord, 28

Taylor, Sir William, 83
Thomson, James (1700-48), 8

Valerie Marie of Schleswig-Holstein, Princess (1900-53), 75-6
Victoria Melita, Grand Duchess of Hesse, later Grand Duchess Cyril of Russia (1876-1936), 70
Victoria of Prussia, Princess (1866-1929), 58, 60, 66
Victoria, Crown Princess of Prussia and Germany, later Empress Victoria, later Empress Frederick (1840-1901), 6, 8, 10, 13, 15-8, 35-6, 47-8, 51-2; wedding, 9; on C, and H's marriage, 20-1, 23-4, 28; and Emperor Frederick III's death, 55; visited by H, 58, 70, 72; on Christian Victor's death, 74; last months and death, 80-1
Victoria, Duchess of Kent (1786-1861), 5-6, 9, 31
Victoria, Marchioness of Milford Haven (1863-1950), 89
Victoria, Princess (1868-1935), 86
Victoria, Queen (1819-1901), 8-10, 12-3, 16, 30-1, 40-1, 43-4, 48-51, 53-5, 57, 60, 85-7, 92, 96; and birth of H, 5; and Prince Consort's death, 11; and Ruland, 15; and H's marriage, 17, 19-29; critical of H, 32; 'bored' with C, 33; and Franco-Prussian war, 36; on H's ill-health, 37, 70;on Marie Louise's ugliness, 38; provides financial assistance for H and C, 45; golden jubilee, 54, 56; considers H unpleasant to family, 61; and C's eye accident, 62-3; last years and declining health, 67, 73-6; and Henry of Battenberg's death, 70; diamond jubilee, 71; death, 77-9; funeral procession, and leaves No 78 Pall Mall to H and C, 79

Wagner, Ernst, 75
Waldemar of Prussia, Prince (1868-79), 42
Warren, T. Herbert, 83
Welby, Lady Victoria, 44
Wernitz, Baroness Bertha von, 76
West, A. William, 84
Wilhelmina, Margravine of Bayreuth, 52
William I, King of Prussia and German Emperor (1797-1888), 18, 22, 50, 55
William II, German Emperor (1859-1941), 46-7, 51, 56, 58, 60, 81, 90; at QV's deathbed, 77, 79; held partly responsible by H for outbreak of war, 91; and H and C's golden wedding anniversary, 92

William III, King (1650-1702), 79
William IV, King (1765-1837), 20
William of Orange, Prince of the Netherlands (1840-79), 10, 18
Winterhalter. Franz Xaver (1805-73), 6, 8, 103

Xenia, Grand Duchess of Russia (1875-1960), 98

ALSO BY JOHN VAN DER KISTE

Royal and historical biography

Frederick III (1981)
Queen Victoria's Family: A Select Bibliography (1982)
Dearest Affie [with Bee Jordaan] (1984)
- revised edition, *Alfred* (2014)
Queen Victoria's Children (1986)
Windsor and Habsburg (1987)
Edward VII's Children (1989)
Princess Victoria Melita (1991)
George V's Children (1991)
George III's Children (1992)
Crowns in a Changing World (1993)
Kings of the Hellenes (1994)
Childhood at Court 1819-1914 (1995)
Northern Crowns (1996)
King George II and Queen Caroline (1997)
The Romanovs 1818-1959 (1998)
Kaiser Wilhelm II (1999)
The Georgian Princesses (2000)
Dearest Vicky, Darling Fritz (2001)
Royal Visits to Devon & Cornwall (2002)
Once a Grand Duchess [with Coryne Hall] (2002)
William and Mary (2003)
Emperor Francis Joseph (2005)
Sons, Servants & Statesmen (2006)
A Divided Kingdom (2007)
William John Wills (2011)
The Prussian Princesses (2014)
The Big Royal Quiz Book (2014)
Prince Henry of Prussia (2015)
The last German Empress (2015)

Local history and true crime

Devon Murders (2006)
Devonshire's Own (2007)
Cornish Murders [with Nicola Sly] (2007)
A Grim Almanac of Devon (2008)
Somerset Murders [with Nicola Sly] (2008)
Cornwall's Own (2008)
Plymouth, History and Guide (2009)
A Grim Almanac of Cornwall (2009)
West Country Murders [with Nicola Sly] (2009)
Jonathan Wild (2009)
Durham Murders & Misdemeanours (2009)
Surrey Murders (2009)
Berkshire Murders (2010)
More Cornish Murders [with Nicola Sly] (2010)
Ivybridge & South Brent Through Time [with Kim Van der Kiste] (2010)
Dartmoor from old photographs (2010)
A Grim Almanac of Hampshire (2011)
The Little Book of Devon (2011)
More Devon Murders (2011)
More Somerset Murders [with Nicola Sly] (2011)
The Plymouth Book of Days (2011)
The Little Book of Cornwall (2013)
Plymouth, a City at War 1914-45 (2014)

Music

Roxeventies (1982)
Singles File (1987)
Beyond the Summertime [with Derek Wadeson] (1990)
Gilbert & Sullivan's Christmas (2000)
Roy Wood (2014)
The Little Book of The Beatles (2014)
Jeff Lynne (2015)

Fiction

The Man on the Moor (2004)
Olga and David (2014)
Elmore Sounds (2015)

Plays

The Man on the Moor (2015)
A Mere Passing Shadow (2015)

Printed in Great Britain
by Amazon.co.uk, Ltd.,
Marston Gate.